2/21/14

To Richard,

I am appreciative of your friendship as well as leadership in the Church. God bless —

BEAMS OF HEAVEN AS I GO

BEAMS OF HEAVEN AS I GO

BY
Willie Woodson and Elizabeth Simms

Enchanters Publishers
Richmond, Virginia

ISBN   0-9787942-0-6

Enchanters Publishers
Richmond, Virginia

DEDICATION

This book is especially dedicated to my mother, Marian W. Winston, a.k.a. "Sister Seay" by her friends and siblings. She was also affectionately called "Goo" by her seven children and friends of her children. A special thanks goes to Mr. James O. Price, proprietor of the grocery store, for whom I worked from elementary school until graduation from high school. My deepest appreciation is also extended to Uncle Edward Seay, my mother's first cousin, who embraced her as his sister, and provided a love and dedication that positively influenced our immediate family through difficult times.

Reverend Willie Woodson
Co-author

Table of Contents

Chapter 1

It was early autumn in Virginia, the season of her greatest beauty, some say. Anticipation rose—from Chincoteague Island with her herons, ospreys, and salt oysters to the Blue Ridge Mountains filled with ancient paths, down which had come the Monocan Indians, Scotch-Irish settlers, Confederate soldiers fleeing their erstwhile Northern brothers, followed at last by vacationing city folk attempting to recapture an ancient yet steadily fading connection with nature, for however briefly, before returning to the numbing rhythm of efficient walks down concrete slabs into brick office buildings with ubiquitous tiny windows and drab curtains. But in every city, village, and town, the old and chilling premonition rose. The harvest was coming. Harvest which ever engenders joy—or dread.

All along the highways, verdant leaves continued to shimmer in the increasingly cool sporadic breezes that always accompany the coming of the fall harvest days. It was no different in Richmond. Monument Avenue glistened in the afternoon sun like the gleaming white shoulders of a haughty belle entering the veranda, snapping her fan open, her eyes darting coquettishly over possible conquests. But the Confederate conquest of an ancient people, of an ancient land, had ended in bloody defeat, a defeat which still rankled the hearts of the little old ladies strolling the Avenue this late September day, their perfectly coiffed white hairdos covered in a sea of straw hats, knobby blue veins popping out along

1

their arms and hands, most of which rested on walking canes. The freshly blooming flowers depicted on their sleeveless summer dresses made silent mockery of their stooped and withered bodies. They smiled bravely and waved at each other, consoling themselves with memories of power, ease, and hope, memories jogged into brightly resurrected visions by the statue of Lee sitting on Traveler, his eyes fixed upon some distant battlefield, a distance they traveled with him every time they passed him by. They would stand, gazing into his face, hiding in the shadow he and his steed together cast onto their uplifted heads.

There he sat, transfixed in time — it was time they longed for, the time they saw in his steadily gazing eyes, time left to fight for a fleeting dream. And they believed — believed they still had time, would always have time. They straightened up a little higher as they passed young mothers with their broods enjoying the fading sunshine on the Avenue. The children deftly skirted them and their cumbersome canes, giggling and chasing each other into the same shadow the women had just vacated, their laughter abruptly stopping as they too fixed their eyes onto Lee's. The old women turned and smiled. Surely the children believed — surely the children would give them time.

But the shadow cast this afternoon reached much farther than the Avenue strollers, and the battlefield Lee sought with his eyes was still intact. Upon its hardened sod, the lifeblood of fresh soldiers still flowed; the bright kindling of vanquished martyrs still briefly flamed and just as quickly expired. But always others entered the fray — always some of the fallen rose up and pressed on.

Far beyond Richmond that day, in the farm country of Millboro, Virginia, a young boy lay dying of pneumonia. Sweat covered his fevered black body like a funeral shroud.

2

Rain was fatal to him—the cold, hard rain that had fallen on his already soaked skin as he had shivered in the back of a pickup truck, the white farmer and his wife inside the cab. They considered themselves exemplary Christians, so when he died later that week, they sent his mother a sympathy card. It was unfortunate, they told relatives. They knew he was fragile from diabetes, which made even a cold all the more dangerous. But surely his mother understood that they couldn't have him sitting in the cab with them. And of course, they didn't go to his funeral. So the mother buried her child. She had eleven other children to console her for the loss of her first-born son.

Welcome to Virginia. They say that Virginia is for lovers. My mother and father were two of those lovers in late 1940s Virginia. Five-feet-two, with hair almost to her shoulders, pretty teeth, and even more beautiful brown eyes, my mother turned heads as she entered the beauty parlor where she worked as a beautician. And so romance blossomed for her very rapidly in the form of a chocolate brown beau sporting a mustache and sculpted muscles. By the spring, she knew that her firstborn child was on the way, a child who would be the first in the family of three girls and four boys.

But as September approached, so did impending tragedy. Two weeks before the birth of her son, her father died. And then as her son came out of the darkness of her womb into the lighted hospital room, the light suddenly went out for her. For two weeks, total blindness engulfed her, robbing her of the long anticipated vision of her baby boy.

I am that baby boy, who came into the light on September 20, 1948. Actually that first light was electric, as I entered this world at night, 9 p.m. to be exact. My mother had her delivery at St. Philips's Hospital, reserved exclusively for black patients under Richmond's strictly enforced racially segregated society.

My mother named me after her father, so I was named Willie, a derivation of William, originally a High German name, "Willehelm," meaning "protection." In the manner of biblical tradition, my name was to serve as a mirror of events surrounding me, and attributes placed within me by divine providence, as I was continually afforded heavenly protection, while being called upon at a tender age to wear the mantle of masculine protector, a mantle which weighed heavily at times on my young shoulders.

We settled into our home, which for us was a house for the larger family of grandmother, three aunts, four uncles, eight cousins in the Navy Hill section of Richmond, where my mother would always dress me in extremely bright colored clothing, due to my dark pigmentation, adorning me in the finest apparel of luminous colors in an attempt to make me look "good and handsome." During the summer days, she would ride me around in her baby carriage, me sporting my brilliantly colored attire, as she dared anyone to touch me or call me "cute"!

What became of the man who romanced my mother? When I reached the age of 3, he left us, leaving us to the man that I truly think of as father, a short, small man whose diminutive stature belied the monumental influence he exerted on the son he raised as his own. Daily, we watched him leave to ply his trade as a shoe repairman, coming home quietly each evening—even the music he listened to was always kept at a low volume. As distinguished and clean-cut in appearance as he was articulate and proper in demeanor, he headed our family with steady strength and dignity, casting a net of security over the entire household with his calm yet protective masculinity.

And so I grew under their guidance, while I was steadily

provided with a growing number of siblings. We played with each other, or with neighboring children, at a nearby playground, often playing in the rain, running jubilantly, the cool wet droplets hitting our faces, eliciting shrieks of laughter. I can remember so vividly one episode of divine protection that was provided me when I was but six years old. I was out playing in what I thought to be the same refreshing rain we always played in, when suddenly the wind increased her intensity to such a frightening degree that I ran towards home, the wind and rain whipping me furiously. Before I had gotten three houses away from my home, I saw a man step on a telephone wire from one of the poles on the street, and I watched his electrocution in horror. I trembled as I swiftly ran into our house, the wind outside continuing to howl and moan like some marauding hungry animal.

We attempted to secure the doors and some of the windows by placing large pieces of furniture against them, but our efforts were in vain. We huddled in the wind-rocked house, my mother and two uncles sheltering my sisters and me in their arms, until the storm subsided and things returned to some degree of normalcy. It was then my mother told me that Hurricane Hazel had just swept through the city of Richmond. The face of the electrocuted man, a face that could have been mine, stayed with me nightly in recurring nightmares.

Then one evening that same summer, a few of us were out late cavorting on the playground when suddenly we heard what sounded like the growl of a ferocious bear, at which everyone scattered and ran for safety. There was a vacant car parked alongside the playground, so frantically, I climbed in and kept hidden in the seat, peering out periodically at scrambling grown-ups and children, some of them shrieking and crying. I lay still on the seat, my heart pounding, until the running footsteps and moaning animal sound desisted.

I tentatively rose up and peeked out; the street was empty and silent, so I darted to a neighbor's house, and after what seemed like an eternity, he answered my zealous knocking. As he walked me three doors down to our home, we shared relief that no one had been hurt, and I was silently thankful for being enclosed a second time in the blessing of deliverance. (I am not aware of who or what caused the sound, even until today.)

The sprawling sun-kissed days of summer lingered languidly, as I cavorted with my sisters on sizzling sidewalks, eagerly anticipating the fall of darkness, when the hum of mosquitoes provided a steady cadence for fireflies dancing silently among us, as we shrieked and played games in pitch-black yards. Some of the boys would pounce on the flies as they lighted, scooping them up into Mason jars, watching them frantically jumping and glowing before being released. But I was content to watch them meander freely through the soft night.

An imperceptible stir began to inundate the thick, still August air. Autumn breezes shook the leaves friskily, and we could hear them shimmying boisterously above us as we hid behind the tree trunks in a game of hide and seek. Then one morning, my mother dressed me in a crisply starched shirt and pants, informing me that my sister would be walking me to a place she called "school" —Navy Hill Elementary School, to be exact. I immediately balked, running into the room I shared with my sisters, slamming the door, and stubbornly sitting by the window with my arms tightly folded across my chest.

I heard the door softly open, and saw my mother out of the corner of my eye pulling up a chair beside mine, wordlessly looking out the window at the same gnarled oak tree that had riveted my gaze, as I continued to sit with my lower lip poked out. My mother just sat there, mimicking my folded arms by folding her own, her lip poking out just like mine. I tried immensely not to laugh, but the sight of my mother sitting there with her lower lip poked down, a mock-serious expression on her face, was too much to try to sit through impassively.

I began to laugh, quick staccato cackles punctuated with brief snorts that stuck in the back of my throat. My mother joined me, our shoulders shaking, and our bodies and heads thrown back joyously, laughing so hard that tears began to run down our already sweat-soaked faces. We blinked at the tears and sweat running into our eyes, till at last I ended our revelry by pulling out the handkerchief from my back pocket, my mother taking it to wipe off our glistening faces.

She hugged me, her lush laughter spilling into the hot, sticky air like refreshing sprays of rain, her soft wet cheek pressing against mine. Suddenly, all the trepidation fell away from me, like a pleasantly dissolving dream. She planted a wet kiss on my cheek, pulling my head onto her ample bosom as she hugged me tightly.

She rocked me in her arms, sweat from her face pouring onto my hair, a peaceful river drawing me deeply into her solacing waters, allowing me to emerge safe and strong at my own pace, in my own time, renewed by the deep recesses that lovingly engulfed me, sustaining me still in the silent communion we shared.

I rose up from her arms and walked to the living room, my bemused sister waiting to walk me down to Navy Hill, which as it turned out, was only a few blocks away from our house. But seeing all the strange faces turning and staring at me as I entered the classroom rendered me recalcitrant yet again, and I ran into a corner, my back to the group of laughing children, my eyes glued to the floor.

I felt a soft hand lightly squeezing my shoulder, and I turned around, staring up into one of the kindest, gentlest faces I have ever encountered. She told me her name was Mrs. Scott, and that she would be my first grade teacher. From that first moment when she tenderly smiled at me, I was the recipient of her relenting patience with my crippling shyness. She had a most difficult time leading me to participate with the other students, whether at play or in class activities. But she persevered, giving me the time I needed to adjust to this strange new group in which I suddenly found myself. She was determined to cajole, to prod, to push me out of my isolated corner somehow. At times I would burst into tears of loneliness and frustration, and she would always comfort me, giving me my own space in which to recuperate until it was time to go home. I grew to love her dearly, and the bond I established with her, along with her expertise in handling my sensitive nature, eventually enabled me to also bond with my fellow students.

She wisely held me back in first grade the next year, assigning me to the same class attended by my sister Zee, one year younger than I. We were an inseparable pair, and with her constant companionship, I loosened up considerably and was finally able to interact with other classmates. We even appeared in a play together, a feat that catapulted me into actual sociability. With my newfound social skills, I also began to excel academically, making all As that year, earning promotion to second grade with flying colors.

My sister and I had a lot of fun that year. I especially remember one warm autumn day when our class went out on a field trip to a dairy farm. We walked to school early, thick white clouds congregating above us in a pink-tinged pale blue sky. We began anxiously running for the school bus that would carry us to another world that day, a world of soft sunshine, shining green fields, and large, comfortably cool old barns with their invigorating smells of earth and hay.

We scampered to the bus, eager for our day's journey to commence, Zee beating me in our race for the window seat. Everyone was anxiously chattering, waiting for the teacher to signal to the driver to depart. Finally, we pulled off slowly, gaining momentum as we turned onto the highway, passing the tiny boxy houses that formed a monotonous single line along either side of us. Children were running and jumping through disheveled and weedy yards, a few dogs chasing alongside the bus and yelping noisily. We passed many more of these shabby houses with their paint peeling down like long traces of tears, the small green patches of yard before them sprouting a few patches of brightly colored flowers.

At last, the houses were replaced by vast green fields, where orders of tall corn stalks shot up like silent sentries snapping to attention as we drove past. We watched muscular black men, donning large straw hats, bending and rising in the cornrows. They glistened in the pouring autumn sun, the color of plump, purplish blackberries ready to be picked, their bodies as taut as the corn ears they plucked fiercely, their bulging arms lustrous with sweat.

It was Indian summer, and though the air was tinged with intermittent cool breezes, the sun was beating down enough to raise a sweat on our faces also, as we poked our heads out the open windows. A group of cows grazed together to our left, and us boys immediately started making "moo" sounds at them, the girls giggling at our ludicrous attempts to sound bovine. Sunlight flickered among the outstretched branches of passing trees, setting ablaze the crimson, burnt orange, and yellow leaves, in fiery contrast to the jet-black branches that sported them.

Suddenly, Zee drew her breath in a startled gasp, and I

9

turned my head to see a large white farmhouse gleaming in the bright sunshine, its forest green shutters coolly framing sparkling windows. The vast lawn was a visual delight — ancient moss-covered oak and gnarly old apple trees intermingled, the long cool fingers of their shadows spreading across the shimmering green grass. Farther off across sprawling fields, we could see the barn, where overalled black men holding silver-colored pails stood conversing with a big beefy white farmer, who wiped his sweat-covered neck with a handkerchief.

Over in the fields beyond the barn, a long brook spanned by a short bridge meandered invitingly. We immediately started clamoring to be let off the bus, and as the driver slowed down and turned off the highway, the teacher shushed us, making us line up quietly and leave the bus in an orderly fashion.

Several men escorted us to the barn, where my class nemesis, Amanda Wilson, immediately began teasing me about my reluctance to go near any of the stalls. I hovered in the corner, while all the other children followed the workers eagerly, hoping to get the chance to squeeze the cow's udders with their own hands. I was overwhelmed with the initial strange stench of the animals, although as the morning wore on, I got used to the earthly smells of the barn and its hay, and began to really enjoy myself.

But for now, I became the target of Amanda's taunts, and just as she would always do in class, Zee immediately advised her that she should stop. Amanda pushed Zee away from her, but Zee climbed right up behind her. She hurried way ahead of Zee, looking down at her from her perch high in a hayloft, sticking her tongue out saucily. Zee continued climbing, but before she could reach the top, Amanda caught her shoe in the top ladder rung, plummeting into the hay below, her straw-covered black legs sticking straight in the air, exposing her bright red underwear and white petticoat, her flouncy red skirt falling around her in the bed of hay.

I started cackling, and the chickens started clucking; Zee (who had hurried back down the ladder to keep from missing this show) and the other children added to the sudden cacophony with shrieks of delight. Our teacher initially tried to restore order, but when she caught sight of Amanda's red underwear, she too succumbed to her own amusement and joined in our laughter. Finally, one of the farmhands climbed the ladder and gallantly rescued Amanda from the hayloft. Recovering her usual haughtiness quickly, she sauntered snootily out the barn door without a backward glance. Yet she never teased me again after that day.

After this little fiasco, the teacher allowed us to let off some steam by going over to the brook. We ran through the fields in little groups of four or five, Zee and I being joined by several other boys. We ran towards the narrow dirt path leading to the brook, yellow dandelions growing in the grass on either side of the pathway. I picked one and stuck the stem between my teeth, as we separated the tall weeds with our hands. Clouds filled up the sky till it seemed more white than blue.

Beyond us, on the other side of the brook, clusters of male and female field hands ambled along as they broke for lunch, laughing raucously at jokes shared among them. One of the men looked over and waved at us, so the other boys waved back. The men and women sauntered on through the field, and though we could still see them in the distance, we could no longer hear their voices.

Several rabbits scurried out of our way, as we began running down the path, anxious to join the others who had by now reached the bridge. Zee and the other boys ran ahead of me, stopping and staring at something lying in the path. I ran up and joined their little circle, looking down at a dead bird whose sightless eyes were fixed on the sky, whose spindly legs twisted grotesquely below its brown body. One of the other boys attempted to pick up the bird, but was shooed away by Zee. He called her a chicken, making buk-buk noises and flopping his arms, but she ignored him and led our way to the others playing by the brook.

We ran back and forth over the little bridge spanning the clear light green water, enjoying the sudden gusts of cool wind that blew over our bodies and created huge ripples in the water. I ambled away from the others, over to a small bench under a tall tree growing near the water. The air was deliciously cool in the shade, and I luxuriated in my new-found and unexpected solitude (something I have always treasured, and when immersed in its healing solace, savor every moment).

I watched the squirrels darting up the tree trunk. The leaves moved slowly up and down with the breeze like lazily fluttering fans. A blackbird descended onto one of the branches, hopped about a few times, then flew away. I leaned back against the back of the bench, and watched the top of the sun rise out of dispersing plump clouds. In the distance, an ugly weather-beaten cabin popped up out of a tangled cluster of weeds, its crumbling roof encircled by a bevy of blackbirds, some of which sauntered sprightly along on the edge of the roof before flying away with the others. I stared at the birds taking off in flight, wondering what it would be like to fly far away over hills, valleys, forests, and mountains, a long journey of kaleidoscopic vistas ending finally on the soft white sand bordering the roaring ocean. I fell asleep, hearing ocean waves crashing on a beach, and dreamed of squishing my toes in wet sand, picking up a smooth pink shell, laying it in the center of my palm, tracing its scallops with my fingers....

"It's time to go, Will!" I looked up into Zee's face bent near mine, her hand shaking my shoulder. I looked over to see the other children lined up behind our teacher, ready to start walking back to the bus. My sister took my hand, and we ran together to join the others, taking up the rear. We basked in our remaining moments in the countryside, wishing we could stay longer, playing by the water in the warm autumn sunshine.

When we got back to school, we had immense fun learning to make butter, followed by a surprise indoor picnic prepared for us by some of our parents for our special day. We had paper plates loaded with deviled eggs, fried chicken, bean salad, potato salad, and cold cornbread, along with ice-cold tart lemonade. We barely had room for the sweet potato pie our teacher had made.

That night, we regaled our mother with stories about our wonderful day, a day that I brought out from memory's treasure trove again and again during the turbulent times ahead, polishing it with precious recall to its original clarity and luster, in desperate need of its soul-sustaining beauty.

But on this night, it had merely been a fun day in the country for my sister and me. And little did I know, but the next day and night would unfold in a swirl of events that left me dizzy.

Chapter 2

———◆———

I awoke early that next morning. One of my sisters was apparently having a nightmare, and she turned and kicked me in my shins repeatedly.

"Hey, Zee!"

"Get away from me!"

I pushed her back towards Jamie who was loudly snoring on her back at the edge of the bed. I kicked Zee on her calf, and she woke up with a start, blinking and staring at the wall.

She sat up, looked down at me, lying there with my eyes closed, feigning innocence.

She whacked me on my head. "You kicked me!" She started raising her leg to kick me back.

I opened my eyes in mock surprise. "Leave me alone! You were just dreaming!"

This seemed to convince her, and she lowered her leg. Jamie continued snoring, her mouth wide open, oblivious to our shenanigans. I took her jaw with my hand, and pushed it up to close her mouth, at which she woke up. Thinking Zee did it, she slapped her, and they screamed and kicked each other, as my grandmother poked her head in the door to call us to breakfast. She marched over to the bed, scooped my sisters up by their garments, and roughly set them on the floor.

"Noise enough to wake the dead in here—and I don't want to see any dead folks before breakfast, do you? Now wash

14

your hands and get on in the kitchen! You too, Little Will."

We crowded around the bathroom sink, running our hands quickly through the water, jostling with each other for the soap.

Grandmother hummed as she set our food on the wooden kitchen table, wiping her hands on her blue-flowered apron. We joined our cousins at the table, and waited while Mama (we sometimes called Grandmother "Mama") blessed the food. I didn't pay attention to her prayer, with aromas of bacon, eggs, potatoes, and apple muffins wafting through the air. We ate with relish (all except my stepfather, who had crept in quietly during the prayer, slowly savoring each bite, meticulously wiping his mouth with one of the damask napkins grandmother brought with her when she came to stay with us.)

She also brought us her culinary artistry, indulging our fondness for homemade rolls and biscuits, as well as the most tender and savory fried chicken and country-style steak—not to mention the best steaming hot cup of strong coffee around. I drank my cup slowly, pursing my lips and blowing waves through the top of the hot liquid before each sip.

"Morning, Ma'am!" A very rotund milky-white insurance salesman appeared at the kitchen screen door, a dilapidated briefcase in one hand, a wide toothy grin on his jowly face.

"Be right there," Grandmother called to him without turning around. She pulled a wad of bills from her bodice, and then went out to pay the collection. We heard the salesman cackling, and I went over to the screen door and peered out.

"There he is—come on out here, Little Will." Grandmother opened the door for me, shaking her head in amusement at the upcoming ritual we performed every time the insurance man came to collect. He walked through the yard, calling me over conspiratorially, and then bent over to talk with me behind a fat bush in the corner of the yard.

"Look at you this morning! Maybe you'd like to get lime-ade to go with your lime shirt!" He jabbed the green shirt I was wearing with his thick fingers and, laughing at his own corny joke, raised up my right hand, laying a dollar bill on my open palm. Then he slapped me on my shoulder, picked up his briefcase, and with a "See you next time" thrown over his shoulder, left me to plan how I would spend my treasure.

Everyone was laughing as I came back into the kitchen. "Why does he only call Little Will? All these children—why this squirt?" My aunt grabbed my nose. "Must be those bright threads Sister always pokes you in!"

I ignored my aunt's teasing, and ran back outside, wanting to be alone with the sky, the trees, and most of all, with the blessed and rare quiet that surrounded me as I strolled through the yard. The sun played peek-a-boo from behind soft white clouds, coquettishly peeping out, and then quickly hiding again. A sudden breeze lifted up several of my mother's faded flower dresses, and they billowed like sails in the wind.

I looked over at our neighbor's yard next door. The Larson children came out their backdoor running through their yard, breaking the precious silence with whoops and yells. Their two dogs listlessly meandered through the grass, sniffing at a cluster of scrappy flowers. Barry Larson saw me and immediately bent over, picking up a rock to throw at me, holding it over his head menacingly. I looked around for a rock to throw back at him, but just then, a group of birds landed on the makeshift fence bordering our yard, so they became his target, instead. He threw the rock, and they scattered, his little sister watching and covering her mouth as she giggled. She ran behind him, towards the apple tree he began to climb, and jumped up onto a branch. Her dress was too big, and the jump made her top fall down her bony shoulders. She squealed and climbed higher.

But then the screen door squeaked open over at the Winstons' house and I forgot all about the Larsons. My heartbeat quickened with the sight of this amber-colored girl in a pink cotton dress wheeling along her bicycle, her long silky chestnut hair cascading around her shoulders. She bent over to flick away a bumblebee that had landed on her bicycle handle. At first, she didn't see me, and she stood watching the Larson children chasing each other around the apple tree. Slowly, she turned her head, and smiled in my direction. She waved, and perching her bike up against a tree, walked towards me gracefully. I watched her face as she approached, a face that always refreshed me with its radiance as much as it intrigued me with its startling contrast of features.

As she neared me, I gazed into her large hazel orbs that overpowered her petite mouth, widening eyes framed prettily in long eyelashes, and appearing voluminous by the time she stood before me. She waited for me to speak, tilting her head to the side, her lips curled slightly in a bemused grin. My shyness always tickled her, since she had not a trace of it, and she had patiently brought me along from our first days together last summer. I had stood at the edge of the yard, watching her peddling her bike back and forth, not moving, tongue-tied to her repeated hellos as she rode by.

But she had decided I would make a fun playmate once she could get me to speak—or even move—in her presence, and she persisted in her quest to break through my wall of silence, with smiles at first, and finally with kisses she would throw at me while peddling by. Her sister Margie often biked with her; she would sail by, the wind whipping her long brown hair into her face. A pretty cream-colored girl, she was not nearly as patient with my timidity as her sister. But she eventually grew used to me being around, and as I blossomed as a playmate under her sister's tutelage, Margie and I became friends as well. The three of us formed a rollicking trio, climbing fences and trees, dodging mosquitoes to play hopscotch, stickball, and hide and seek.

But it was Kookie Winston who captured my heart, which was beating briskly now as she stood before me, sweeping her hair back from her face with her slender fingers.

"What are you up to today, Willie?"

I shrugged my shoulders. "What about you?"

She pursed her lips. "Well, I was going to ride my bike, but since you don't have one—" her pensive face brightened with an idea. "Mother's making gingerbread. Why don't you come over, and we'll play in the yard till it's done?"

"I'll ask Grandmother," I called out, already running back through our yard to the kitchen door.

Breathlessly, I charged in. "Mama!"

She whirled around from the sink, and shot me a look, her hands on her ample hips.

"Calm down, boy. What's got you so riled up?"

She peered out the window at Kookie.

"So that's it. Yes, you can go see your gal—but if you do, you'll miss your Uncle George. He was going to take you with him this morning. The other children are going, and your cousin Huck, too."

Uncle George was driving to Petersburg this morning, and had told mother we could ride along, and then go back to his house for dinner and a sleepover with our cousins, Huck being my favorite, as she was one year older than I and we were very close.

I was usually eager to go places with Uncle George, a

powerful man who worked hard but always had fun while he worked, with his lively sense of humor that smoothed over any mishap life would throw at him. I had gone out with him a few times this summer on his ice wagon. He was as enterprising as he was good-humored, and always combined business with pleasure, selling this or that as he socialized throughout all the neighborhoods in our area.

Everyone knew Uncle George, and I was proud when he pointed me out as his favorite nephew to beaming adults who would offer me a lemonade in summer, coffee or hot chocolate in winter. I drank quite a few lemonades that summer, watching in awe as he chipped a large block of ice in half, deftly carrying it up rickety steps to some neighbor's icebox.

He made me feel very grownup, leaving me to care for the wagon while he delivered ice—and his colorful stories—to enthralled housewives. I was uncomfortable doing this at first, since he used a horse to pull the wagon, and I'd never been around such creatures before. I was afraid the horse would take off with me in the wagon and I would end up flung into some neighbor's bushes before I could rein him in. But the horse was well trained, and always waited patiently for Uncle George, flicking his tail at the circling flies.

We sat in front of each house while Uncle worked his spell. Finally, he would come bounding down the steps, or rise up from a chair among women shucking corn on a porch, or burst through a kitchen door, two huge slices of homemade cake tucked in wax paper dangling from his hand.

Some lady would always want to see the "favorite nephew," and I would watch her waddle out to the wagon in a flowered sleeveless smock, smiling down at me proudly. My cheeks were pinched, my forehead was kissed, and I was handed lemonade, cake, or cookies. Then off we would go, till we circled the whole area, arriving that evening back at the stable, which was midway down the block. Tired but satiated with good food, I helped by cleaning the ice wagon while Uncle George brushed the horse and fed him hay. "One day, you'll have your own business, Little Will," he would tell me, instilling in me quite early a perpetual search for entrepreneurship.

"Well? What's it going to be? Hurry up, child, I've got things to do." Mama impatiently waited for my decision, her arms folded across her checkered apron.

Without hesitation, I informed her to tell Uncle George hello, but I would be over at Kookie's.

"Well then, let me get you a loaf to take to Mrs. Winston. She brought us some lemon cookies yesterday—you can have some later."

Mama was a domestic worker and seamstress, a trade she learned in New York, where she traveled all her young summers to be with her father. At this time, she was working at the John Marshall Hotel in downtown Richmond, about a quarter of a mile from where we lived. She always brought home sundry bread loaves for us to try. We were regularly treated to raisin, rye, wheat, and pumpernickel, as well as savoring occasional onion, cranberry nut, and honey oat.

Sometimes she would tell us little stories about the breads, the countries where they were originally eaten, or which kind was liked best by various rich and prominent people dining at the hotel. But my favorite story was how pumpernickel bread acquired its name. Mama told us that pumpernickel was a course rye bread made from unsifted flour that "a lot of German saddity-folk originally looked down on." She said, "Nickel" was the name of a German goblin and when he "pumperned," he was breaking wind. "So after you eat this, you'll sound like little goblins passing wind!" And sure enough, after we ate the bread that morning, Mama was proved to be right, as usual. "Little goblins breaking gas," we teased each other as we succumbed to the predicted flatulence.

"Now there's one loaf of onion, and one of pumpernickel," Mama told me. "And here's her plate back. Now, you get yourself back before supper. Your Uncle Billy's having his rowdy friends over tonight—something you wouldn't have to worry about if you went with George."

I ignored her warning, and ran across the alley to the Winstons' backyard. Kookie had climbed up on the limb of an old apple tree while she waited for me. As I neared the tree, I looked down at the napkin-wrapped loaves, laughing inwardly at a vision of the Winstons flatulating all evening. A wide grin broke out on my face.

"What's so funny?"

"Nothin'. Mama sent this bread to your mother. And here's her plate back."

She jumped down, and ran to the kitchen door, which squeaked as she opened it. Mrs. Winston stuck her head through the door and waved. When Kookie came back out, Margie was with her. She was the older of the two, and much taller. She pulled her dark brown wavy hair back into an impromptu ponytail, whispering something in Kookie's ear as she did so. Then she mischievously stuck her tongue out at me as she passed, running to her bike and peddling down the road.

"Looks like it's just you and me. Margie wanted me to ride with her down by the pond, but I've seen enough of those ducks this week." She sighed. "I get tired of the clucking chickens as it is."

As if on cue, a covey of hens suddenly emerged from the side of the house, clucking and circling a bantam rooster,

21

who strutted and preened regally, accepting their homage as his just due, before bending his small head to peck at some kernels in the dirt.

"Hush up that fuss! Shoo!" Kookie yelled at the hens as they skedaddled towards the porch, where Mrs. Winston stood throwing feed from her gingham apron pocket.

"Kookie, you and Willie come on in the kitchen—ginger-bread's ready."

The smell of the freshly baked bread lavishly spiced the air as we hurriedly washed our hands in the sink, before plopping into two of the wooden chairs at the table.

The screen door squeaked open, and Mrs. Winston stepped in, setting a large bucket of eggs on the counter. She was still fresh and beautiful like her daughters, despite the sunup to sundown toil that sustained her family after Mr. Winston had died suddenly five years ago. She wiped her hands on her apron, her long wavy hair pinned up in a tidy bun, her huge expressive hazel eyes perfect replicas of Kookie's. She stepped regally over the faded yellow linoleum floor, wearing the serene smile of a lady of leisure, just come in from a stroll through lush shaded gardens.

Kookie got up from her chair to help her mother serve the gingerbread. She brought the pan over to the table, running the knife around the edges of the bread, then carefully cut three thick slices, while Mrs. Winston set glasses of iced tea on the table. Then her mother eased into her chair gracefully, and bowed her head in silent grace.

I sunk my fork into the moist bread, inhaling the strong aroma. It tasted as delicious as it smelled, and I luxuriated in each bite, planning to take an extra piece home, if Mrs. Winston would let me.

"When did you get up, Mama? Sorry I overslept."

"Oh, way early, child—when the sun wasn't even thinkin'

about shinin' yet. And oh, what a beautiful sky! We had a walking sky this morning, you know."

I wrinkled my forehead.

"I see you don't know what that is." She laughed. "A walking sky is when the clouds hang so low, so thick, and so puffy white, you feel you could just climb into the sky and walk barefoot all through them. That's how the sky was early this morning."

Kookie secretly made a face at me, snickering at her mother, who was always studying the clouds, or the birds, or even the crawling caterpillars, as she did her chores, humming softly, gazing off in the distance, some mysterious secret knowledge lighting up her eyes. She had briefly taught school when she was younger and she would read some of the poems she had written to us. Kookie, with her pragmatic mind that charged every child a nickel a head to see her seashell collection, would only roll her eyes at her mother's "silly sayings." But I was fascinated with stars that turned into jewels, and sunsets that became kisses of angels (although I could also be just as practical as Kookie.)

"Willie, you'll have to excuse us now. I need Kookie to go with me to sell the eggs." As her mother cleared the table, Kookie dashed into the living room, signaling me to join her for our usual ritual with the music boxes. She would wind all the boxes that sat on a corner table, one of which she used to store her little trinkets—a marble, a pebble, even a duck feather. She picked up a pink lacquered box topped with two pinkish-white swans and wound it, doing the same with each of the boxes, as we listened contentedly to the tinkling notes overlap into a joyous jumble of myriad melodies.

She clapped her hands together and laughed, liquid laughter as sweet to my ears as the music. "My Aunt Vinnie had an antique store, and mama would take us there sometimes. She had cuckoo clocks, grandfather clocks, and music boxes—all sounding at once! You would have loved it, Willie!"

She looked at me, pursing her lips, her forehead wrinkled in thought. She picked up the swan music box, the one that held her treasures, and took out a small object. "Close your eyes and hold out your hand." I complied.

"Now open them."

I looked down at my palm, and there lay the robin's egg blue pebble she had found down by the creek. I felt my heart pounding in my chest, surprised that she would give this valuable keepsake to me, as she had mentioned it being her favorite.

"Kookie, time to go! Willie, come get a piece of ginger-bread for later."

"We're coming, Mama." As she turned to go back to the kitchen, she suddenly whirled back around and kissed me on the cheek. My heart was racing, as Mrs. Winston appeared, handing me the bread and taking Kookie by the hand, es-corting us out the front door. I stood watching them cross the yard to the street, Kookie turning around and waving me good-bye.

I walked around the side of the house and cut through the backyard, crossing the alley to our house, whistling and throwing my pebble up in the air, catching it and turning it over and over in my palm, staring into its cool blueness. I could still feel Kookie's soft lips on my cheek. It was the only one she would ever give me, as the Winstons moved to another section of Richmond before the fall was over. Later my family would also move—often and all too suddenly, all over Richmond. But now I was ecstatic from her kiss and her gift, walking through the yard as cocky as the rooster strut-ting by the fence.

"Hey, Little Will. Got anything for me?"

I turned to see Mr. Floyd standing by his truck, holding a box load of junk our neighbor had given him. Mr. Floyd was an interesting character to me, a man who turned rags and rubbish into the large sums of money he flashed before us children, who stood bug-eyed with wonder as he peeled off bills as nonchalantly as we pitched pennies. I was amazed he could make this tidy of a sum selling our junk to the dump, and I decided I would be a seller like Uncle George and Mr. Floyd when I grew up—what I would sell I hadn't determined yet. But I wanted to turn junk, or ice, or anything into a large wad of money, so I could pass out dollar bills to the children, and watch their faces light up.

"No, Mr. Floyd," I called to him. "No box for you this week." He got in and revved up the truck, which was full of boxes on both seats and in the bed. With a "catch you next time," thrown out the window, he gunned the motor noisily, peeling off down the alley, leaving a trail of thick smoke from the exhaust pipe.

I turned and looked up at the sky, which could have inspired one of Mrs. Winston's poems. A fleet of billowy clouds sailed slowly past the sun, harboring together in an ethereal sea of pale blue. Grandmother was out by the clothesline, hanging her floral aprons, swept up and sent to flapping in a swift cool breeze.

"My, my, look at you," she teased. "You look like the cat that just swallowed the canary. What's that in your hand? Don't tell me that little tomboy knows how to cook now!"

"Gingerbread. Mrs. Winston made it."

"Hum. Needs to be teachin' that gal to cook instead of wasting time lookin' up at the sky. Saw her the other night— middle of the night, at that—my rheumatism had woke me up—standing smack in the middle of her yard, lookin' at the stars like she was in a trance. Don't get me wrong—God wouldn't of laid out the stars so sparkly and pretty, if He didn't want us to admire them sometimes. But there's a time and a place for everything." (Grandmother's favorite expression, and behind her back, I mouthed the words along with her.) "Neither one of those gals can cook! Got to teach them young. Shoot, I was burnin' when I was knee-high to a duck. There comes a time when folks have to eat, and when your plate's empty, all the stars in the sky can't help you!" She picked up the laundry basket and started inside. "Is Mrs. Winston gonna cook for their husbands, too? Better hurry up and introduce that tomboy to the kitchen now! Get this door for your grandmother. And another thing...."

On and on she expounded on the Winston deficiencies as she walked through the door, setting the basket down on the kitchen floor and puffing, holding her right shoulder with her left hand. "Lord, if I could get my hands on that doctor, I'd kill him! 'You need to move back down to Virginia, get away from these New York winters,' he says. Young boy—wet behind the ears—young people don't know their backsides from their fronts. Go on back outside and play. I've got to lay down."

Whop!

"What was that?" Grandmother peered out of the window, scowling at some intruder, her hand still holding her shoulder. (When grandmother's rheumatism acted up, we automatically knew three things—she would be evil for a day or two, it would rain in a day or two, and we would all stay out of her way in the meantime.)

"Oh Lord, what is he doin' here?"

Whop!

I was out of the door, but could still hear her through the window. "I wish your mother would stop lettin' that man come here. They should of given him ten more years for misplacin' his brain—stabbin' a man over that no-good Watson girl."

She pulled open the screen door and called to the bare-chested man chopping wood by the tool shed.

"Purcell Brown!" He never looked up. "Purcell Brown, you hear me! I got my eye on you!"

For a brief second, their eyes met in silent mutual revulsion. "And don't be caterwaulin' any of those old chain gang songs—you ought to be singin' to the good Lord—He's the one who delivered you from where they should of left you!" He continued swinging his axe, impervious to her verbal knife twisting. She turned and went back in the house.

"Help us, Lord."

I sat under the apple tree next to the shed, watching Mr. Brown split the wood, sweat drops glistening on his body, lean and muscled despite his years, which were revealed in his crop of white hair. Due to his gruff demeanor and Grandmother's stories, I always kept my distance, but was intrigued with this mysterious figure and the plaintive, strange songs he would sing while mending the fence, chopping wood, or pulling weeds. None of the adults cared for him, but since my stepfather worked long hours and didn't care for the yard work, my mother had assented the day he came looking for odd jobs to do.

So I watched him from the shade of the tree, waiting to hear his deep baritone rising in the stillness. It was an unusually warm day, even for Indian summer. The sun was rising from behind a cloud, the kind of sun Mrs. Winston called a "black coffee sun"— "steaming hot and pouring down strong."

He worked steadily, his face expressionless. He glanced up at Grandmother's bedroom window, where she stood frowning and pulling down the shade. He smiled impishly, raising the axe roughly, sounding his voice as loudly as he could.

"It was one Sunday mornin'—Lord, Lord, Lord.
The preacher went a huntin'—Lord, Lord, Lord.
 He carried long his shotgun—Lord, Lord, Lord.
 And along come a grey goose—Lord, Lord, Lord."

On he sang about a resilient goose that survived the saw-mill, the hog pen, the knife and fork, finally escaping and "flyin' 'cross the ocean." He pulled out a handkerchief from his back pocket and dabbed at his face, looking up at Grand-mother's window.

He began humming as he chopped, then emitted a long soaring moan that pulled me into an unbidden vortex of emotion, overwhelming in its intensity, from which I emerged in complete visceral kinship with Purcell Brown. I rose up in the cool shadows of the tree, transfixed by this virtual stranger splitting wood in the autumn sun.

He closed his eyes and swung down the axe. No longer spiting a contentious old lady, he railed against a more ancient nemesis:

"Go down, Ole Hannah—"

Whop!

"Honey, don't you rii-ise, don't you rise no more—"

Whop!

"If you rise up in the mornin' baby, won't you bring down the judgment day—"

But the sun still climbed cruelly in the sky, just as it had over hosts of nameless black men in fields, on railroads, with chain gangs, swinging their scythes, their axes, their hammers, as the brutal sun reached its zenith; a fiery spear aimed relentlessly at bartered black bodies, searing their flesh and piercing their souls with its thrust, their lifeblood flowing in feverish hollers and shouts, vain entreaties for respite rising up to an impervious and merciless orb.

"Wake up, dead man, grab your hoe—"

Whop!

"Wake up, dead man, 'cause your buddy's too tired to row."

He sang of men, but I knew from listening to the older folk that women and children worked right alongside the men in the fields, their souls just as thirsty, their voices rising just as strongly, in the rows of corn, cotton, and tobacco. I saw their faces, heard their moans.

"Wake up, daddy, do your peas—"

They came towards me now, tramping wearily, specters eternally quickened in the notes of a work song—

"Hey, Willie! Come on in here! Got something for you."

I was relieved to hear Uncle calling to me from the backdoor, releasing me from my disturbing reverie. I passed Mr. Brown, who had stopped singing and was preparing to leave.

"Is your mother here?" Mr. Brown asked.

I shook my head no, as she was still at the beauty parlor.

"Tell her I'll be by Monday evening for my pay." With that he ambled through the back fence gate and slowly walked down the alley. "Oh Alberta. Oh Alberta," he called, as children bicycled by, oblivious to his passing.

I ran through the door, and was immediately scooped up by Uncle Billy Buck, who held me high over his head, twirling me 'round and 'round at a dizzying pace, till we both fell in a tumble on the kitchen floor. Then he began tickling me, and I began squealing like a pig on the killing floor, causing him to place his fingers over his lips, cautioning me not to wake up Grandmother.

Grandmother and Uncle Billy (his real name was Richard—why they called him Billy Buck, I never knew) couldn't abide each other. So they had made tacit agreement to circle around each other, settling down to parallel territory, like a cat and a dog lying at a safe and respectable distance from each other in a baking hot yard, lethargic but wary, any closer contact resulting in mutually inflicted scratches and bites.

Uncle pulled me up from the floor with one strong hand, then sat at the table, his large frame barely fitting into the hardback chair, like a teacher sitting at one of his first-graders' desks. Everything on Uncle Billy was big—hands, feet, arms, legs, chest, neck, even his strong beautiful nose. He sat drumming his fingers on the table, full of the restless energy that propelled him through life.

Perfectly formed curling eyelashes adorned his expressive brown eyes, without adding the slightest trace of femininity to his round pleasant face. Nor did the long scar running down the right side of his face take away from his magnetic appeal. He wore the scar proudly, a fleshly badge of honor arduously won as a paratrooper in Korea.

Oh yes, the women took to Uncle Billy Buck, this big, scarred, mercurial, restless man with his quick, decisive manner and off-handed humor, disarmingly nonchalant one minute, surprisingly ardent the next. They thrilled to hear his voice, rich and deep as a mighty river, regaling them with a story or joke, punctuated by his mellow infectious laugh as they basked in his glowing vitality, their brown eyes sparkling like the wine in their cups.

They flocked to him on porches, in darkened corners of strobe-lighted yards, even on church steps in the bright Sunday sunlight. From the plump, bun-topped matron to the littlest double-Dutch champion in bows and braids—he held them all in sway. There they would stand, girls in their best flowered frocks, heads cocked to the side, furtively stealing glances at his broad back, his smooth black skin shining like polished leather. "Good morning, Mr. Billy," they would casually greet him, hiding quickening hearts, hoping for a bright smile back from him, waiting expectantly to hear his deep voice bestow a compliment. And any compliment was cherished privately, repeated publicly among themselves, amidst anxious hair twirling and dreamy eye closing, punctuated with heavy sighing.

Chattering coteries of young women swayed by, seemingly oblivious to his presence, lightly jostling him. Apologies dipped in powdered sugar dropped from their soft lips— "Why, I didn't see you, Billy"—followed by furtive glances to see if they had lit a gleam in his eye as they oozed past, praying he hungered for more of their proffered sweetness.

But the true connoisseurs of Uncle Billy were the more seasoned matrons, with unmarried daughters, nieces, and granddaughters. All envisioned the beautiful babies he could bestow on their family, if only they could ensconce him, by means of culinary lures, in blissful matrimony with Sally or Sue or Pamela.

These were the cooking sisters, the queens of their kitchens and houses, towering regally above all the subtle subterfuge of their younger rivals. They forthrightly stood toe to toe with Uncle, blocking his path. "Why Billy, have you lost weight? How long has it been since you've had a good home-cooked meal? How about coming to dinner next Sunday?"

Each had her own unique vision of Uncle sitting at her own exquisitely set table, enchanted with a daughter's smile, a niece's hourglass figure, but always—and mainly—enticed into the family with what everyone knows to be the best macaroni and cheese, fried catfish, or sweet potato pie in Richmond.

Uncle Billy, who loved good music, good laughter—but

especially good food—would thank them for their kindness, and accept many an invitation offered him by the ladies on the church steps, at which they would beam and proudly descend past envious competitors, buoyant in anticipation of capturing such a fine eel with their gastronomical bait. And he would deftly snatch the bait without getting caught on the hook, quickly and silently swimming away to unexplored waters.

Today was no different. As soon as he pulled up in his 1949 Holiday Coupe Oldsmobile, curtains were pulled back and unseen eyes followed his slow exit from the car, his regal stride down the walk to our front door, his light blue suit contrasting pleasantly with his ebony hue.

And sure enough, as Uncle was letting me throw down his brawny left arm in a pseudo man-to-man hand-wrestling match on the table, came the traditional soft knocking on the screen door that always attended his arrival.

"Yoo-hoo! Marian? Are you there?" queried Mrs. Turner, a youngish widow from down the street (knowing full well that Mother was still at the beauty parlor). I opened the door for her, and she entered, sweetly smiling and holding a pie, feigning surprise at seeing Uncle. "Billy! I didn't know you were here!" She slanted her eyes in his direction. "But my— aren't you a sight for all the sore eyes? Where's Marian?"

"She's at the beauty parlor today," Uncle informed her, adeptly playing his part in the mating ritual.

She placed a beautiful orange sweet potato pie down on the table, her eyes shooting furtively on Uncle's broad back as he bent over, inhaling an aroma from the pie, an entranced smile on his face.

"Well, Little Will, since your mother's not here, I'll just leave this with you. Tell her I enjoyed the rice pudding." She stood with her hands on her hips, her head tilted to the side coquettishly, waiting for Uncle's invitation to join us at the table.

"Little Will, get three plates and forks," he finally request-ed. He winked at me as she eased her wide girth into the chair across from him. I sat down next to Uncle, sinking my fork into the silky orange filling, watching as they ate in mu-tual silence, accentuated by the loudly ticking clock on the wall.

Mrs. Turner closed her eyes and "Hmmmed" over her own concoction, her breasts rising and falling in counterpoint to the ticking clock. She glanced at Uncle over her horn-rimmed glasses, which had fallen halfway down her nose. She was a striking woman, yellowish-brown complexion, queen-sized, with soft shiny curls cascading down to her neck. But her pretty face had filled out over the years until she was left with several chins. As she ate, she continuously blinked her small brown eyes, which resembled little choco-late chips stuck in her doughy face. She watched wordlessly as her nuptial prey finished his pie, finally returning her gaze nonchalantly as he set down his fork.

"How was your pie, Little Will? Was it as good as Grand-ma's?"

I pondered a moment. "Yours smells better, but Grand-mother's tastes better."

Mrs. Turner bristled, and Uncle Billy howled at my seven-year-old lack of diplomacy. But all was forgiven as he quick-ly took her hand, squeezing it gently, promising to come to dinner Thursday night. She rose from the table, extended her hand to Uncle, who placed it to his lips in a gentlemanly kiss. Then she floated across the kitchen floor and out the door.

"A little romance—and now we're gonna dance. Listen and learn," Uncle told me, as he turned on the radio. The station always played oldies from the 40s and early 50s on Saturday, and he would show me all the old bebop steps. A trumpet pealed, as sweetly as church bells, followed by a girlish voice, exuberant in the first flush of romantic love, dipping into full womanhood amid blaring trumpets and pounding drums. He cavorted around the room, blending his voice with the singer's. "You speak and the angels sing"— his sonorous delivery coupling perfectly with the woman's delicate crooning. I mimicked his steps, closing my eyes, and popping my fingers.

"You got it Willie, you got it."

We glided across the room together, dipping and twirling in the pure joy of synchronized rhythm, joy fading quickly like the trailing horns of the song, as Uncle's friend Milton burst through the door without knocking, slamming it shut, cases of beer bottles under his arms, more beer, whiskey, and wine on the porch.

"Hey there, Willie." He pulled his huge lips back into a long lopsided smile, his ragged yellowish teeth appearing like half-chewed corn-on-the-cob. I nodded my head at him, cringing as he overzealously slapped me on my back. He began snapping his fingers and circling the table, mingling his off-key harmony with Nat King Cole's mellow vocals, pairing with Uncle as they glissaded across the floor to the refrigerator.

They made quite a pair—Uncle Billy, a short, squat, but devastatingly handsome firecracker, with tall, nappy-headed Milton, gangling and goofy. No one else in our family liked him, not even us children, who found his boisterous antics more asinine than amusing. But Uncle found him funny, so he frequently cast him as his elongated shadow. (Grandmother said it was also because Milton didn't appeal to women, leaving more for Uncle).

34

They carried all the liquor in together, laughing raucously and exchanging mock insults, Milton slamming the screen door shut behind them.

"Lord, help us! A lady can't even get a cup of tea in her own house without running into hooligans! What is this old world comin' to? Don't you know how to close a door?" Grandmother had emerged from her room, the sight of Milton and Uncle setting her off like sparks landing on dry wood. She stood with her hands on her plump girth, glowering at Milton. Never taking her eyes from his, she opened the door again and closed it gently. "This is how you close a door!"

"Well, ma'am—and I don't mean no harm—" he tried awkwardly to be slightly ingratiating—"that is how you close a door, for sure. But I'm just a big ole country boy, and I like to hear my door make some noise! Just like I like to hear my woman make—"

"Hush that!" Grandmother glared at him reproachfully, cocking her head in my direction. "You see that child? You better be glad you didn't finish that sentence—I'd box your ears!" With that, she pushed him back and took her kettle to the sink to fill it with water. "And if Marian didn't need the money from your revolving-you-know-what house you call a party, I'd throw you both out right now!"

Uncle frowned as she hobbled over to the stove to heat up her kettle. He didn't give a fig what she thought of him, but he didn't like to hear anyone belittle Milton, though they frequently heckled each other. The two sat at the table, uncomfortably silent, drinking cold bottles of beer, as Eartha Kitt softly purred "C'est Si Bon."

I watched Uncle slipping into one of his melancholy funks, his eyes staring blankly at the kitchen wall, his fingers tapping restlessly on his thigh, as he jiggled his leg under the table. For once, I was glad Milton was with us. He was the only one who could grab Uncle on his descent into the blues, pulling him up with a joke or prank before he fell completely immersed within a turbulent—potentially violent—emotional maelstrom that no one, save Milton and the most ardent or foolhardy of Uncle's devotees, could endure.

This was the side of Uncle Billy not all of his female admirers had seen (and the hapless recipients of his rages didn't bother spreading the word, as misery endlessly loves company). Within the family, of course, his alter ego was a frequent visitor, especially after he or one of our bootlegging cousins held one of their soirées.

One night last spring, my sisters, cousins, and I had an encounter with this other Uncle we'd never forget. We came up with the sage idea to follow him as he went out on some nocturnal romantic rendezvous, hoping to catch him smooching on a bench, or caressing in the shadows. He'd turned around quickly, sensing someone was following him, at which we all scampered behind some bushes. But one of my cousins tripped, and Uncle turned back around in time to see him sprawled in the grass. He came over, his breath reeking of gin, and scolded us, warning us to return home. We agreed, but secretly continued following him, to be caught and sternly warned several more times.

The third time he caught us, he escorted us all home, lining us up in the front room to receive strikes from his belt. Since there were six of us, I moved to the back of the line, thinking he'd be exhausted by the time he got to me, allowing me fewer licks. My cousins and sister Jean screamed as he belted them, surprisingly garnering some sympathy as he momentarily relented, and they each received only two hits.

Unfortunately for me, he then came to my sisters Janie and Zee, who goaded him with their defiant faces, stubbornly refusing to whimper as he thrashed them all the more. Smirk-

36

ing as he reached his last victim, he whipped me with relish, and though I knew I should have whimpered like Jean did, I followed the example of my other two sisters, receiving the same protracted thrashing that they did.

"Let's see you peeps scope out your Uncle now!" he laughed, as he buckled back up and headed out the door, leaving us huddling in pain on the sofa.

So I was actually relieved when Milton started mincing across the floor on his toes, in grotesque imitation of feminine pulchritude in heels, intoning "C'est Si Bon" in a piercingly high falsetto that set Grandmother to gritting her teeth and rolling her eyes.

This revived Uncle, who clapped his hands and made a wolf whistle as the teakettle also started whistling. Grandmother quickly poured hot water into her cup and retreated back to her room, shaking her head and Lord, Lord-ing.

The song finished, and Uncle stood up, slapping palms with Milton. Glad to see him back in a jocular mood, I got up and did a slow drag to Ruth Brown's "Teardrops from My Eyes."

"Go ahead, boy—show us old men how to do it," Milton called to me between sips of beer. "Say man," he turned to Uncle, "is that Larson girl down the street comin' to the party tonight?"

"You're askin' about the string bean?" Uncle sighed. "I told her about the party, so I guess you two string beans might end up in a casserole together before the night's over. Me—I got my eye on Sadie. Knew she'd be back some day." His face softened momentarily.

"Sadie—yeah, now that's a gal that's—" Milton curved his hands in the air to demonstrate Sadie's form. "Coca-Cola bottle, right, boy?"

"Coca-Cola, for sure," I agreed, trying to sound very

grownup.

Uncle rolled his eyes at me. "Now what're you doin' peepin' out curves, Little Will?"

I grinned sheepishly, remembering Kookie's wet kiss on my cheek.

"Shoot, when I was his age—" Milton started.

"You're still his age—up here." Uncle tapped Milton's forehead with his fingers.

Back and forth they went, joshing each other while the radio blared bluesy boogies and fervid torch songs. I was being initiated into a world of men radically different from my stepfather's. They were bustling with life, and in my child's mind, vastly outshone his quiet demeanor. For years, I was held in their sway, the steady beacon of my stepfather's life obscured as I walked into increasing darkness, allured by these lesser lights, flashing with greater intensity, glowing with the flush of wine and whiskey at dusk-to-dawn house parties, fish fries, and joints. It was only during my spiritual conversion, a long eclipse later, that I clearly saw the glorious light that stepfather continued to beam into the deeper recesses of my soul.

But this afternoon, I was bedazzled with my first tastes of the sporting life. And I could think of nothing better than trailing Uncle through his debauchery, side by side with his two "shadows," the other of which stood knocking at the door, the smell of trout already filling the room. Sherwood, the other member of Uncle's ubiquitous trio, was a natural composite of his two cohorts—tall, lanky, and jocular like Milton, good-looking, fickle yet magnetic like Uncle. All of us liked Sherwood, even Grandmother.

"Already cleaned and ready to go. Get to burnin'!" He handed the wrapped trout to Uncle, who motioned him to get himself a beer from the icebox.

Uncle got out Mother's iron skillet and began frying the trout. Grandmother had made a pot of greens this morning, so he warmed them up also. Sherwood shuffled across the floor, a bottle of beer in hand, snapping his fingers to the Wolf's gravelly lament, wafting through with the air along with the savory aroma of fish and greens.

"O-Oh, Smokestack lightnin'
    Shinin' — just like gold
Oh don't you hear me cryin'
A-ooh-ooh — "

"Let me hear you, brother man," Milton chimed in, beating on the table in unison with the drummer.

Uncle set down the plates of steaming hot food before us, along with more ice-cold beer all around — and a glass of iced tea at my plate. We ate with gusto, sinking our teeth into the succulent crispy fried trout. Uncle studied me a minute as I ate, then handed me his bottle of beer. "Take a swig — just a few swallows."

I hesitated. "Go ahead — what are you, a baby?" my two other "Uncles" coaxed me (Uncle insisted we children call his two companions "Uncle"). I took the bottle, and gulped the wonderfully bitter brew down my throat. I attempted to guzzle some more, but Uncle grabbed it from me. "That's enough for now — we'll set you up later at the party."

I took my tongue and rolled the cold foam from the brew all over my lips. We ate without talking, sharing food, drink, and music in silent male communion, the older men belching and swigging down their beers in between bites. Finally, they leaned back in their chairs, satiated and ready to jostle, to spar, to one-up one another — to be men together, away from female intrusion.

Milton leaned back till his chair touched the wall, his head rolled back, his eyes closed, rocking his chair to the pounding piano boogie. He leaned forward, the front chair legs giving way, his long body hitting the floor in a grotesque sprawl. The swelling peals of our laughter joined with his own, as he raised himself up, dramatically holding on to the tabletop with both hands. He was obviously on his way to inebriation, as were the other two men.

We sat listening to the music, which had mellowed into a Roy Brown blues. I sat listening to the men, enthralled with the exchange of good-natured expletives, and stories of romantic exploits, the details of which I didn't completely understand, making them all the more intriguing to my novice ears.

"Oscar was by the river last week with Carrie Wilson. Wonder if he caught anything? Besides fish, I mean."

"Shoot, Sher," (they called each other Sher, Mil, and Bill), "Oscar couldn't catch a cold!"

"Saw her sister Marla at Carrie's fish fry last month. Looking mighty big in the stomach." Sherwood narrowed his eyes, and stared into Uncle's face. "Course you wouldn't know anything about that."

Uncle let out a short whoop of a laugh. "Sure wouldn't. Been a year since I climbed those mountains." He stared back at Sherwood. "But I hear you went mountain climbing last spring."

Back and forth they went—while I was still in hopes of being given more of the magical potion that bonded men together in song and laughter. Afternoon was imperceptibly turning to evening, and the paling sunshine streamed through the window, casting a surreal circle of light onto the center of the table.

I went over to the icebox to get more tea, and stood for

a moment looking out the backdoor. Children were out on the sidewalks jumping rope, peddling bicycles, and playing hopscotch in the softly pouring sunshine. They chased after chickens, dogs, and cats, fed pet rabbits and turtles, before their mothers called them in to dinner. Overhead, thick clouds began to disperse into thin white strands threading gently through the pale blue sky. I stood sipping my tea, enjoying Ella's "Smooth Sailing."

"Alright, man, we'll see you around 9. Later, Little Willie."

Sherwood and Milton slapped me on the shoulder as they brushed past. Uncle sat at the table, nursing his bottle of beer, turning it slowly round and round in his hands, staring at the circle of light on the table, growing smaller as the sun neared its setting.

He lay back in his chair, his eyes closed, head cocked to the side. At first, I thought he had fallen asleep, but suddenly he began humming—a bittersweet and pungent murmur that rose and fell with the flapping window curtain.

"That's Martha White flour—" The announcer's voice was jubilant as he broke incongruously into Uncle's doleful utterance. "For the flakiest biscuits you'll ever eat!"

For the only time in my life that I can remember, I actually yearned to hear "Uncle" Milton bust through the door again, to feel him slapping me way too hard on the back. If he didn't return till nine, it would be too late, and tonight would be "that kind of party."

Ever since I could remember, we always had two kinds of Saturday night parties. One party consisted of a jocose upbeat Uncle Billy, entertaining family, friends, and females with gracious aplomb and contagious joie de vivre, with everyone not only intact, but actually elated as night turned to dawn. The worst brawlers at this party were a couple of drunks exchanging words over a stepped-on toe, a spilled-on drink, or a stolen-from girlfriend—handled immediately and adeptly by Uncle and his two "shadows," acting as unofficial bouncers.

The other party (to which I feared we were quickly descending) revolved around a rowdy, morose Uncle Billy, lambasting anyone within earshot with an arsenal of insults, stealing women (married and single) from various escorts, and with the help of his two cronies, defying any male objectors to do anything about it. It was at this party that men's fists were used, female rivals' wigs were pulled off, and knives—even Saturday night specials—were sometimes brandished.

It was for this very reason—this "other" party—that my stepfather always vacated the premises on these nights, going over to his brother's house after dinner, a safe retreat where he could play chess, listen to Bach's "Air on the G String," or read DuBois essays. Grandmother, who could sleep through a hurricane, ensconced herself in her room early, just as she did today, not to emerge until time to make breakfast before heading off to the early church service. Neither murder nor mayhem would rouse her—though she often warned that any of Billy's rowdies entering her room would be greeted with "lead between the eyes."

Mother herself, though allowing Billy's parties out of pressing financial need, didn't care for them and didn't like us children to attend. She would often take us over to stay with our cousins for the night, which is where my brothers and sisters would be staying tonight, since they all went with Uncle George.

Although Mother and Stepfather made enough to tide over a smaller family from month to month, a family as large as ours needed the financial supplementation from extra odd jobs, and the sale of eggs and homemade cakes and jams.

We children sold lemonade, shined shoes, and took empty bottles back to the store. And Mother reluctantly let Uncle Billy (the brother of my real father) have his parties and fish fries at our yard, for a much needed cut of the proceeds. So she gritted her teeth, sternly admonished any remaining children to stay upstairs, and silently prayed all day that Uncle would be in high spirits when she got home from the beauty parlor.

So I watched Uncle with trepidation, the clock loudly ticking on the wall behind him. I picked up a lemon from a white bowl on the table, dropping it into my tea, which was good and strong and not too sweet. I thought about this morning and Kookie's soft kiss on my cheek. I still had the gingerbread her mother gave me, planning to eat it later with some milk.

Kookie's mother! It dawned on me that there was one other remedy for Uncle's funk besides Milton—the prospect of a new flame. Besides, if it worked out, I would have even more chances to be with Kookie.

I took a swig of tea, cleared my throat, and made my pitch. "Say Uncle, you remember Kookie—the girl I play with sometimes from across the street? The one with the red bike?"

Uncle stared ahead impassively. He thought a moment. "Oh, yeah. Real light. A real looker too. All that long hair." He punched me in the side. "Got you goin', don't she, boy?"

I smiled. "Well, you know, Mrs. Winston, she's a real looker too—and her hair's mighty long when she takes it down. I've seen her brushing it—the sun comin' through the window makes it shine. Her, her husband died—"

Uncle began laughing. I joined him, thinking I had paved the way to many supper invitations from Mrs. Winston. He eyed me over his beer bottle, "That gal's got your nose wide open, don't she boy?" He jabbed my shoulder with his finger. "And you figure if you get old Uncle hooked up with Mama, your little crush will be part of the family—kissing cousins, huh?"

"No, I—"

"Is she a good cook?" he went on, ignoring my protest.

"The best—just like Grandmother!"

He snorted, "That's supposed to reel me in?" He paused, "Say, wait a minute, is that the lady that brought over the peach cobbler last July?"

I nodded, thinking I had cinched the deal.

"Oh man—" he began shaking his head vigorously. "No—no way. I mean, she can make you think of walking her down by the river, but I'd be the only one walking! I can see us now, my arm around her, her gazing up at a cloud—" He laid his hand on my arm, sensing my disappointment. "She's up in those clouds, Willie—and I don't have it in me to get those two pretty feet to touch the earth. You understand? I have to have a woman who walks beside me on God's green earth. You'll understand when you get older. Now that gal you like—she's an earth walker, and if she was just ten years older," he gave me a sly smile, "you wouldn't stand a chance!"

I smiled back. Though my original plan had fallen through, I took his teasing as a positive sign that his mood had lifted.

And then I saw her—saw her before Uncle did, as he had his back to the door. A nicely shaped leg dangling from under a red skirt, dipped in sheer nylon, swung inside the backdoor, followed by another shapely leg, belonging to a beautiful—and I mean, beautiful—woman, her short curly hair accentuating her large brown eyes, her finger to her red lipsticked lips signaling me to be quiet, as she tiptoed up to Uncle's chair.

"I saw the harbor lights—" she crooned along with Dinah. Uncle sat there a minute, dazed, the familiar voice obviously shaking his insides, lending a surprising and seldom seen fragility to his face. She stood there waiting for him to turn around, winking at me and wearing the confident smile of conquest.

He closed his eyes, all expression leaving his face, as he composed himself for her perusal. He got up slowly, looked her in the eye impassively, and then walked past her into the backyard. She threw her head back and laughed, a delightful laugh that sent a small shiver through me. She helped herself to a beer from the icebox, and then followed Uncle outside.

I was intrigued, but I knew better than to show my face outside when Uncle was with a lady friend, having been backhanded by him the night my sister and I hid in the shrubbery, watching him kiss Melinda Thomas for twenty minutes straight. So I eased over to the window, standing just to the right of it, peeping out at Uncle and the beautiful brown-skinned lady, standing under the apple tree, drinking their beers. The lady's liquid laughter poured sweetly through the air as she stroked his ear.

I slipped over and opened the icebox, looking at the glistening ice-cold brown bottles of beer. I hesitated—Uncle never let me take more than a sip or two, but I gauged he'd be tied up with the beautiful woman for quite a while. I grabbed a bottle and sat at the table, taking tiny sips of the stolen ale. Uncle's laughter rose in the air, along with the woman's. Emboldened with how things were progressing, I took a big swig, the cool foam bubbling on my lips.

My Uncle and the lady strolled past the door; they were joined at the hip, their arms circling each other's backs, her head leaning on his shoulder. They were headed towards a large oak tree in the far corner of the yard. I got up and stood

45

by the sink, to the right of the door, from where I had a clear view of the tree. Fat fingers of pink spread through the blue-gray sky, as the sun descended slowly.

Uncle pulled a little flower up from the grass and handed it to the woman. She stuck it behind her ear, and then pulled him closer, kissing him. I took out the pebble from my pocket, turning it over and over. The Winstons always went over to Mrs. Winston's sister's house for dinner on Saturday nights, so I wouldn't see Kookie till tomorrow. I felt oddly lonesome—maybe it was the beer.

I jumped at the sudden soft padding out in the hall. Grandmother! I quickly stuck my hand out the door and set the bottle behind a bush. I turned around right before she entered the kitchen, grateful that she hadn't seen this gesture. She came up beside me, staring straight ahead at the couple, still embracing under the tree. To my surprise, a low rumble of laughter issued from her closed lips.

As she stared at them, I wiped my mouth of any froth residue, hoping my breath didn't smell like Milton's always did. I walked over to the sink, wanting to get as far away from her as possible, without arousing any suspicion. I began washing an already clean glass.

She went over to the stove, retrieved the teakettle, and then joined me at the sink. She filled the kettle with water, swaying back and forth, while Sarah Vaughan languidly intoned, "I Love The Guy." I was amazed, but continued swiping the glass, as she did a little trucking step across the floor. This was obviously a mistake, as she grabbed her back, bending over and Lord have mercy-ing.

I ran over to her, forgetting to turn my mouth the other way. "Are you alright?"

"Course I'm not alright. Give me your hand and help me to the table!" We hobbled across the floor, and she sank her big frame into one of the chairs, puffing like a locomotive pulling into the station. The kettle whistled, and I brought her a cup of tea, then sat down next to her. She blew onto the hot liquid, then eyed me over her cup as she took a swallow.

"Your breath smells like a speakeasy, you know what I mean?" I shook my head, staring at the table.

"Look at me, boy!" she thundered, as I snapped my head to attention.

She looked at me long and hard without saying a word. For several minutes that seemed like an hour, we sat there. Finally she spoke.

"You think you want to be like Uncle Billy, don't you? Oh, he's so exciting, huh?" She narrowed her eyes, sipping her tea, then her lips spread out into a contented smile. "You don't want to be Billy, son—not tonight, not any night. But tonight—Willie, tonight," she repeated emphatically, "Billy's gonna get skinned alive!"

This odd pronouncement sent her into a menacing cackle that ended in a spasm of coughing tears running down her cheeks.

"You alright, Grandmother?"

"Hmm—Grandmother's better than alright! I only wish I was well enough to keep watching!" She limped to the door and looked out, clasping her hands together, and stomping the floor with her foot. Then she closed her eyes and threw her head back, raising her face in ecstasy, like an ancient prophetess receiving a vision.

She crossed the floor unsteadily, waving me away as I attempted to assist her. "Go on, boy! I don't even want to smell your foul breath! Go brush your teeth!" She turned, and looked fiercely down into my eyes. "And no more beer! Think I won't know—I'll know. Nothin' wrong with these carrot-eatin' eyes. I can see owls blinkin' at midnight!" She walked a few steps, and then turned around again. "And bring that bottle of beer behind the shrub in here — pour it down the sink — I'm gonna stand here and watch you. Now!"

I retrieved the bottle, convinced that Grandmother had extra eyes she kept hidden from the rest of us. I poured the liquid down the sink, listening to it effervesce, while she watched me steadily.

"I'll see you in the morning. Go upstairs tonight, away from the kitchen!" With that she turned to go back to her room. "Thank you, Lord, thank you!" she called, as she slowly made her way up the hall. I watched her till she closed her door, wondering what it all meant.

The front door closed to, lifting me from my musing. Mother came into the kitchen, leaning over and kissing me on the cheek, her familiar kiss and spicy perfume comforting to me in my bewilderment. She stood spreading her soft curly hair prettily around her neck. Falling evening shadows brushed softly across her face, lovingly caressing her smooth brown skin.

She plopped into a chair, tired but smiling. "What are you doing here, Willie? I wanted you to go with your Uncle George. Oh—" she answered her own question, "you saw your little friend, didn't you?" Without giving me time to answer, she chattered on. "Now if you had gone with the other children, you wouldn't be stuck here with us old folks. The others are sleeping over, you know."

"Good! I'll get the bed all to myself! I'm tired of Zee kicking me."

"You're a mess, Willie," she laughed. "Well—we've got to get a move on and get set up. Where's Billy?" She sprung up, having gotten her second wind, and started taking bowls of food out of the icebox, setting them on the counter. She picked up the pot lid and set it back noisily. "Who's been in the greens? Billy's gang." (Mother always answered her own questions.) "Say, where is he, anyway?" she asked me again.

I peeped out the door, but he and the woman had disappeared. "He was here a few minutes ago. "He—"

"Went off with some gal. Leave me to set up, all the work, but he'll want half the profit. Some fool gal—"

She fretted on, as she dashed into the pantry, a cake plate in each hand, setting them down adroitly on the table. "Willie, get the plates and forks. She sighed, "I don't even want to be bothered with these folks tonight. If he pulls this tonight—coming in here late, four sheets to the wind—this is the last party! I know we need the money, but I'll sell every stick in this house. I'll—"

"Whoa, Sis! (Uncle always called mother 'Sis' when he wanted to annoy her.) "People in hell needin' ice water don't carry on like this!"

She whirled around, intending to give Uncle a tongue-lashing. She froze, looking beyond him to the woman who was attempting to light up a cigarette. Mother bristled. "Miss—as Billy full well knows—I don't allow smoke in this house!" Her every word dripped with vinegar, as she continued glaring at Uncle, while the woman slipped her shiny gold cigarette case back into her purse, unmoved by Mother's growing anger.

"Come on, Sis, you know once we're jammin' tonight this kitchen'll be full of smoke!"

The woman let out a husky laugh. Mother ignored her. "That's tonight. The party hasn't started yet! No party, no smoke!" she repeated forcefully.

Uncle said something under his breath to Mother, then turned and whispered something in the woman's ear. She grinned contemptuously at Mother, then slowly stepped through the kitchen, and back out the screen door, her red high heels clicking, her hips swinging under the tight cloth of her skirt.

"Willie, get my purse." She was going to send me to the store for sodas, so she and Uncle could hash out their differences without me listening. I didn't want to leave, but knew it would be useless to protest. She handed me some bills from her wallet, but Uncle snatched them out of my hand. "You stay here with your mother and help her set up. Sadie and I will get the sodas."

Sadie! The mystery woman was the one he'd told us he had his eye on. I was elated, thinking the party would now be sensational, despite Mother and Uncle's momentary squabbling. He pulled Mother's arm gently. "Everything's gonna be alright. Sadie's not half as bad as you remember." Then he sauntered out the door whistling. So Mother knew the mystery lady! My curiosity rose, as we got together meats, cakes, and freshly baked pies, flavoring the air with their pungent spices, as Eckstine crooned "My Foolish Heart." I let Mother cool down some, then I asked her, "Who is that lady with Uncle?" She added another wine glass to the collection on the table, letting out a deep sigh and closing her eyes in response to my question. She continued setting out glasses as she told the story.

"I was pretending not to recognize her. She's older, but it's her all right. Same blood in her eye. Get out the toothpicks and napkins for me, baby." She continued, " Shortly before you were born, at the end of that summer, a family moved in down the street—Sadie's family, the Watkins. The first two years, nothing happened. She was a skinny thing—she looked like an upside down pencil, kept her hair piled up too high for that little head to carry. Anyway, all of a sudden, when she got to be around sixteen or seventeen, I guess, she—well, she didn't look like a pencil anymore. She looked more like a Coca-Cola bottle—you know what I mean?"

I nodded, remembering Milton's words.

"Anyway, Billy was coming over, visiting like always. He had a Studebaker that year, wore a blue sharkskin suit—just back from the war, so he was anxious to cut loose. I'll never forget that day—your uncle had just parked his car, when she came swingin' herself down the street, in her sleeveless black playsuit, the spittin' image of a Coca-Cola bottle and your Uncle took one look, and child, from that moment—" She shook her head. "Her hook's been in Billy ever since. Don't care if she left town, don't care if he's had a hundred women since then—that hook's still in him, tearing up his insides. That's why he's never been able to get hooked by anyone else—he's got to get her hook out first. And now, here she is, Miss Sassafras—" She took a fork and jabbed it into one of the pickles she was setting out on a plate. "She's half the reason we have to suffer with Billy with his evil self."

She grabbed me by my arms, kneeling to look me straight in the eye. "Don't ever get hooked on a girl like that, Willie—a girl with a shark's eye—they've got a frozen heart, and they can get you killed! That's right," she lowered her voice, "your uncle almost got himself killed by a man over that no good gal! That's 'cause Billy don't believe in anything but himself, so he needs to make himself a little goddess, so he can have someone to believe in, someone to worship. So he made sure he picked someone he couldn't have, so she'd always be beyond his reach. That way, he wouldn't have to walk side by side with her—'cause if he did, he'd find out she's just flesh and blood like himself, and not a goddess at all. That would be too much, because then he'd have nothing left, you see?"

But her words confused me, and I didn't see at all. She squeezed me tight. "I'm so sorry. This is talk for when you're older. Mother just needed to express herself. I've been holding it in a long time. What I'm saying is—you believe in the Lord, Willie. You believe in Him. Don't worship any woman, not even me! Okay?"

Not comprehending, I nodded my head yes, as it mattered so much to her that I understand, and I just wanted to see her happy again. She continued. "And when the time's right, the Lord will send you a good wife that you can love and walk side by side with—flesh and blood like you, but also with a good spirit like you. I know it's in you—that's why I named you William. William, that means protection. The Lord will always protect you, son. And you've got to protect yourself from girls like Sadie. You remember that—always remember." She hugged me again, and rose up smiling, as if relieved of a burden shouldered too long.

Uncle came back in the door, with six-packs of soda under his arms, which he set on the floor next to the ice chest. "You two go on. I'll take it from here. Everything looks great—and smells even better." He kissed Mother on the cheek, hoping to placate her. And she actually gave him a peck back. Yes, this was going to be a wonderful evening, I knew.

"Let's go out on the porch awhile, Willie. Then we'll go upstairs and eat cake and play pitty-pat."

I followed her through the living room, switching on the radio that was on the end table next to the door. We went out on the porch and sat in our rockers. (This was one of my favorite pastimes, rocking with Mother on the porch. She had bought me my own small rocker from the thrift store.) Our chairs squeaked as we rocked together, enjoying the mildly warm October evening. Several stars appeared above us, tiny little sparkles in the cobalt blue sky. Across the street, standing at the edge of Mrs. Turner's yard, three young boys melodized a wordless, bittersweet tune, hanging the final note triumphantly in the air for several minutes—human bells, sublimely ringing in the swiftly approaching night.

Other eager young groupings paced the sidewalks, or clustered restlessly under trees and next to fences, drinking wine or soda, laughing and jabbering. The mournful whistle of a train sounded in the distance. Old people, lovers, the shy and rejected, sat protected on shadowy porches, which allowed them their private share of the evening.

Heads turned at two male voices loudly broadcasting their arguments from a beat-up Ford, whose screeching tires peeled down the street. Sherwood pulled up behind Uncle's car, Milton at his side, in the throes of a heated discussion. They got out and sauntered up the sidewalk, curses turning to laughter, as they apparently settled whatever frequent but short-lived dispute they were having. They came up on the porch, nodding to Mother and me. "Hey, pretty lady," Milton flirted with Mother (Milton was always flirting with Mother, having tried unsuccessfully to date her since they were teenagers).

"Blue does agree with you. My, my, yes." He looked her over, his large bulbous eyes popping out of his oblong head.

Mother played oblivious. "Go on, you two, and get yourself something to eat. There's plenty of food."

"Okay, okay, I can take a hint. That's alright—Milton will have plenty of fish to fry before the night is over."

"Then how come you're always the fish who ends up in the pan?" Sherwood interjected.

"Oh, man, why don't you—"

On they went, as they headed back to the kitchen. Uncle and Sadie emerged through the door a few minutes later, strolling arm in arm down the walk from his car, conspicuously profiling for the neighbors. Wolf whistles suddenly sprinkled the air, as young men turned away from their girlfriends to watch Sadie wiggle back up the walk in her tight red skirt. Feminine reprimands spread down the street, although many a girl's eye had surreptitiously rested on Uncle's physique. Mother rolled her eyes as they came up the porch steps.

"Hey there, beautiful. I've always said I've got the prettiest sister in town." Uncle took Mother's hand and kissed it, as Sadie slinked through the door, away from Mother's barely concealed venom.

"And who might that be? Lord knows, a jackass has more relation to a peacock than you to me!"

"Now see, that's cold. We need to warm your Mother up, don't we, Willie? And since I'm not cold like you—" he produced a wine bottle from the brown bag he held— "I got some of Erroll's homemade peach wine for you. Unloose you a little bit. Jaws getting too tight lately!"

"I don't need wine to unloosen me. Just give me Joe Liggins and watch me work!" She stood up and did an impromptu boogie. Uncle nodding his head approvingly, "Still got it, Sis, still got it."

"And I'm gonna keep it!" She suddenly grabbed the bottle from him. "But I'll still take that peach wine."

"Knew you would!"

"Be right back, Willie." Uncle opened the door for Mother, who seemed to have forgotten we were to go upstairs and play pitty-pat. But Uncle always had that effect on people— he made them forget things. Mother would be furious with him one minute, relishing his vivacity the next. And I was glad that he was coaxing her to unwind a little—she worked so hard.

So I was content as I rocked and watched the misty grey of

evening quickly turn into the lavish blackness of night. Cars pulled up, delivering our guests, who patted me on the head and shoulders as they passed by, a hodgepodge of strong colognes and perfumes mingling unpleasantly with their already liquor-tinged breath.

Mother, Uncle and Sadie came back out, Uncle pulling up a chair next to Mother, Sadie vamp-walking down to a hard-back chair at the other end of the porch, where she sat with her legs crossed, blowing smoke rings into the air. Uncle handed me a glass of iced tea, winking and cocking his head towards Mother. "I tried to get you the go-ahead for some bubbly, but your mother's an old lady now."

"No, I'm a smart lady," she rejoined. "No wine before it's time." Disappointed as I watched the wine gurgling up the sides of their glasses, I asked her, "When will it be my time?"

"When you're thirty years old." Sadie loudly snickered from the end of the porch; Mother raised her glass to Uncle, expectantly posing for a toast. Then they clicked their glasses together and drank.

"Now that's good country wine," Uncle declared. "Some of this stuff from the grocery store," he shook his head, "might as well be drinking sarsaparilla."

"Sarsa-who?" Milton stood in the doorway, handing two plates of food to Mother and me.

"Buy yourself a dictionary, man."

He placed his hand on his chest, popping his eyes out at Uncle. "Milton doesn't need big words. Milton's got big—"

Mother shot him a withering glare nodding in my direction, at which he skulked back inside.

"Mom, you can burn!" I told her, smacking my lips as we ate fried chicken, greens, baked beans, and corn bread.

Domino's "Fat Man" sounded from the backyard, "Come

on, pretty ladies! It's a sin to sit down on Domino!" Uncle motioned us to go around back. "You too, Willie."

"Can I, Mama?"

Whether due to the wine or Uncle's persuasiveness, she motioned me to join them. "Just for a little while." Surprised to see her joining the revelers, even for a short duration, I ran to her side. We went around the side of the house, and sat at one of the folding tables Uncle had set up in the backyard.

Darkness poured over us thickly and evenly, like molasses dripping from a spoon. Stars ignited one by one, hanging a dazzling necklace of light across the beautiful black expanse of night. Voices tossed through the air amid rippling waves of laughter, rising to clamorous peaks of cackling, then dipping into soft mellow peals. Cars steadily rumbled through the alley, their headlights intermittently lighting up the shadowy figures milling about in the yard, amid the soft candle-glow from the tables. Myriad couples, full of wine and whiskey, spilled out through the yard, strolling arm in arm, entwining under trees. Boisterous laughter turned to drunken shouting as a slowly cruising car high-beamed groping couples all along the fence, sending them scampering like startled deer.

Someone turned the radio up, as couples still gyrated to "Fat Man."

"Dance?" a man simply asked Mother, who flashed her wedding ring at him in reply. He shrugged his shoulders and withdrew, settling for a tall, skinny lady whose smile revealed an overbite. A raucous tune with a blaring saxophone jumped through the air, picking up feet and sending them flying. The music abruptly ended, then smoothed out into Eckstine's silky importuning of "My Destiny." We watched couples slow-dragging in the grass, Uncle holding Sadie tightly as they swayed languidly by the edge of our table.

"Whoo! I got to get away from that woman!" Milton and

Sherwood plopped down beside me fanning their faces with their wide-brimmed hats. "Too much woman for me, too much," Milton continued. He felt his side. "I think one of my ribs broke!"

They cackled and Mother and I rolled our eyes at each other. "Here we are."

Milton cringed at the sound of the woman's voice, and Sherwood snickered. A very portly brown-skinned lady with a cute though double-chinned face appeared at our table, carrying a round tray of filled whiskey glasses, which she set before the two men, squeezing her wide girth into the chair next to Milton. "Whew—it's hot for October!" She sat fanning her face with her hands, peering over at Mother and me.

"I'm Shirley. And you?"

"I'm Marian, and this is my son Willie." The music changed to "Cuban Mambo," and Shirley grabbed Milton's hand, pulling him out into the grass. Though not a handsome pair, they were energetic and lively, moving gracefully together with flourish. "Go ahead, Mama," one of the younger women called to Shirley, as Milton began showing off for her, clowning and flapping his arms.

"Shake it, but don't break it, please!" Sherwood called to the thin young woman with the overbite, now dancing by herself. She motioned for him to join her, and he jumped up, doing a few mambo steps just as the song finished. Then Little Ester's sexy solo mingled provocatively with the pounding rhythm of "Cupid's Boogie." The woman wiggled her narrow hips daringly, pulling her skirt up above her bony knees, as she made her moves quickly. Sherwood kept pace with her, agilely kicking his huge legs out in a wide leap, then gracefully landing in the grass. They created a stir among the other dancers, who shouted them on.

"Pop those hips!"

"Cut his mouth out, mamma!"

Meantime, Milton gave his friend a run for his money, as he and Shirley maintained their own coterie of onlookers, with their spirited gyrations. The two pairs sat back down at the table, as the other dancers re-coupled to "Blue Shadows."

"He keeps up pretty good with me," Shirley announced. "Don't you, baby?"

"I thought you kept up pretty good with me!"

"And who's the lady that can keep up with Milton?" Uncle asked as he and Sadie joined us at the table. He mopped his face with his handkerchief, beads of sweat glistening in his short-cropped hair.

"I'm Shirley—Shirley who surely keeps up with Milton!"

Uncle took her hand and kissed the back of it, sending her into a fit of giggles.

"You ought to stop that, man!" Milton griped.

"Oh! I believe my man is jealous!" Shirley preened, Milton wincing as she turned her head and took another drink.

A beefy man in plaid stepped up to the thin lady (who never did say her name, not that anybody, including Sherwood, asked). "Dance?" She immediately acquiesced, and Sherwood indifferently watched as he escorted her back into the group of dancers.

"Looks like I've been moved to the back burner," he half-heartedly complained.

"You're slippin' man," Milton told him. "Cut out by a big smoked pork-butt in a plaid suit!"

This set everyone to laughing, including Mother, who had gotten sleepy from the wine. She poured the last of the peach wine into her glass. "We'll go play pitty-pat after Mother finishes her wine," she informed me, resting back in her chair, looking at the stars glow in the coal black sky.

"My glass is empty, baby." Sadie held up her glass, tracing the rim with her red nails. "Go get me some bubbly, will you, sugar?"

No sooner had Uncle gone through the kitchen door than the wolves started circling. Sadie stood up and walked over to the apple tree. Men who had been standing with their drinks in their hands, chatting and watching the dancers, whipped their heads around simultaneously, their eyes fastened on Sadie, like roosters eyeing the same kernel of corn. She leaned against the tree trunk, slipping a cigarette between her lips, then fished in her purse for her lighter. Before she could light up, several young men bounded over, circling her with their lighters proffered, but she waved them derisively away. They ambled away, choosing other partners for Dinah's rendition of "Harbor Lights."

Shirley eased her large frame up out of her chair, her hands on her hips, her head bobbing as she fussed Milton into another dance. "Now why are you folks sittin' around like you're at an ice cream social? Shirley came to dance!" She grabbed her recalcitrant partner, squeezing his skinny frame close to her large body, as they swayed next to the table.

Several slow jams sent Mother to nodding and Sadie, who had rejoined us at the table, began tappin' her foot restlessly, visibly annoyed that Uncle hadn't appeared with her wine. Louis Jordan's "Blue Light Boogie" jarred Mother awake, as Sadie slowly stood up, leaning over to light another cigarette, brandishing her full breasts, spilling out from her low-cut leopard-print bodice.

She caught the eye of a tall thin light-skinned youth standing near the hedges, puffing on a cigarette, his hat cocked to one side over his left eye. She held his gaze, as he flicked the butt away, the ember glowing eerily in the grass. She smiled as she passed us, walking over to the youth, her even white teeth framed in heavy red lipstick. He took her hand and guided her to the head of the body of dancers, easily synchronizing with her slithery cavorting. Remembering Grandmother's words, I gaped at them, transfixed by a vision of Uncle cutting his smiling young rival in shreds. Mother, woozy from the strong wine she usually drank only at New Year's, stared blankly at the dancers, incognizant of the night's fresh taste turning sour faster than buttermilk.

Sadie tossed her hair as she gracefully moved her body. Though not as good a dancer as her partner, she swung her full hips and raised her skirt over her long, shapely legs, swiftly capturing attention. Female eyes shot daggers as their men visually pounced on her, consuming her figure, her face, her saucy eyes full of teasing and defiance. Her partner watched her display belligerently, rapidly growing weary of her toying. They were a troubling pair, charging the convivial atmosphere with a nasty undercurrent.

I wanted to stand up and scream "No!" but I could only sit there, not moving a muscle, sweat pouring down my face. I hoped he would lead her back to our table before Uncle got back, but as "Pink Champagne" began, he pulled her to him, enjoying it when she tightly pressed the length of her body against his. Her head was turned our way, and I know she saw Uncle as he reached our table, two glasses of wine in his hand, his ashy face silently signaling his fury. She fondled her companion's ear, whispering into it, and laughing. He brushed his lips across hers, and she met them in a kiss.

Uncle set down the glasses and walked slowly towards his prey. Sherwood was still inside and Milton was obviously soused, swaying on Shirley's bosom with his eyes closed, like a child sleeping on his mother's breast. Mother lay asleep in her chair. I held my breath and said a silent prayer, my heart pounding in my chest.

Uncle plowed through a cordon of men lining up on the sidelines to openly ogle Sadie, hiding her momentarily from his view. He stood for an infinite few minutes, a semi-circle of men ringing him on either side, staring insolently at Sadie's face, while she eyed him back in bemused derision. The young man began backing away, hesitant, wanting to run, not wanting to appear a coward in front of the other men.

"Please, God," I whispered.

The other couples stopped dancing, riveted to the ground like statues in a graveyard. Everyone at the tables was silent. Dark figures along the far fence crept through the yard to get a better view. Dogs began barking. The radio continued to play "Pink Champagne." Everyone waited.

Finally, Uncle reached out and grabbed the youth's shirt as he attempted to bolt.

"Please Lord." My eyes were open, my palms pressed together, my fingers extended upward. Sadie backed away, leaning against the trunk of an oak tree by the fence. Uncle dragged the man several feet with one hand, holding him by his silk shirt, his wing-tipped shoes grazing the grass. Then he reached for a half-empty beer bottle lying in a tall clump of weeds, breaking it on a metal chair set under the tree earlier by an amorous couple. The golden liquid sputtered ominously onto a dry patch of earth.

He laid the jagged edge of the bottle against the man's throat tauntingly. Sadie, unflinching until now, shuddered and closed her eyes. The youth dangled in the air, held up by Uncle's powerful left arm, his shoe tips brushing the tops of the weeds, his eyes fixed on the bottle, sweat pouring down his taut body. With all his resolve, he kept himself from moving, from swallowing, his Adam's apple pinned in just under

61

the sharp glass aimed at his jugular.

I continued my prayer, my eyes never leaving the trio of dark figures under the tree. Uncle looked up into the man's eyes as they lost all vestiges of fear, meeting his tormentor's eyes stoically. He involuntarily gasped as Uncle raised the bottle up in the air, then swiftly brought his arm down to his side, hauling the dangling youth over to Sadie, dropping him roughly at her feet.

"You- can- have- her," he whispered hoarsely in his rival's ear, bending over his crumpled body, the broken bottle still in his hand. Never looking at Sadie, he stood up, passing the stunned and quiescent flock of men all along the fence, opening the gate and closing it softly, his receding form winding tipsily up the alley.

"Thank you, Lord, thank you, Jesus." My lips formed the words against the backs of my hands, as I lay my head over in my lap. Mother slept in her chair, her mouth open, making low snoring sounds in her throat. The circle of men now broke up into clusters, their voices rising excitedly in exuberant relief from the tense vigil they had been forced to keep, while a strange and savage pas de deux nearly ended in death.

I shook Mother till she woke disoriented, startled to be seated in the backyard with "Billy's rowdies."

"Come on, Goo," (mother's nickname) I said, "time to get upstairs."

She slowly stood up, and taking my hand, we walked through the kitchen door, past a few older men seated at the table, oblivious to our presence. We walked up the stairs to Mother's bedroom. She started to undress, then fell back on the bed, still looking fresh in her blue frock. I took her shoes off, and covered her with a lightweight blanket, kissing her cheek. "Mama," I whispered, thinking of my faithful grandmother sleeping peacefully in her room, "you were right.

Prayer is victory."

I closed the door, and then went back downstairs to the front room. To my surprise, Uncle had returned and was sitting in the easy chair in the corner. Several men lay dozing on the sofa, their glasses of whiskey sweating on the end table. I should have known better than to approach him, but the spiritual power the prayer had released was overwhelming, compelling me to speak of the presence to which I had pleaded. A presence Who had just turned death into life.

"Uncle—I've got something to tell you."

He didn't respond. He was drowsy, but not asleep.

"Uncle—I need to tell you this—it's important!" I blurted.

He looked at me. "Alright, let's go over here."

He led me to the loveseat across the room, and we sat down. He leaned towards me, and spoke confidentially. "Before you begin—there's something your Uncle needs to tell you."

"What is it?" I naively asked.

He leaned over again, whispering in my ear, his words slow and even. "Don't- ever- bother- a- sleeping- dog!" With that, he threw me over his knees with one hand, and proceeded to take his belt off with the other. Confused and furious at the malicious treatment I was receiving following my victorious intercession for him, I nevertheless lay still and didn't whimper, just as stubborn as on the night he'd whipped all of us. He lashed my arms, legs, and backside. Fiery arrows shot through the small of my back as he brought the belt down again. I bit my lower lip with my teeth to keep from groaning, knowing Sadie's face was in Uncle's eyes as he belted me.

Finally he stopped and walked out the front door, leaving me lying face down on the loveseat. The men across the room snored on. I sank to my knees on the floor, panting, my hands tightly clasping the sofa cushion. "Why Lord?" I took several deep breaths, pulling the air greedily into my lungs. I braced myself against a downpour of dizziness, and as it subsided, I slowly stood up, wincing from the pain. My bowels coiled up and rumbled, a stream of pink vomit shooting up through my mouth and onto the rug. I wiped it off my lips with the back of my hand, rising up, and walking stiffly through the hall to the kitchen.

Two men still sat at the table, amid half-eaten cakes and pies. "What's wrong with you, boy?" one of them asked, his slurred words bespeaking his drunkenness.

I didn't answer, leaning over the sink and splashing cold water on my face.

"Come here, son," the same man called to me. I went over to the table, and sat down. The man's companion looked through me, as if I wasn't there. The first man roughly set a shot glass in front of me, and filled it from his bottle.

"Drink up—good for whatever ails you," he exhorted me.

I picked up the glass, and poured the whiskey down my throat, hoping to get the bitter taste of vomit out of my mouth.

"Whoa, fella—not so fast! Ain't the last shot of whiskey in the universe settin' here, you know!"

The radio emitted a female voice I didn't recognize, her song a mellow concoction drawled in honey-dipped tones that soothed me like a soft, perfumed woman sidling up, running her soothing fingers over my frayed nerve endings. I swayed dreamily.

He handed me another shot. As I grabbed it to douse it down, he took hold of my arm. "Sip it. That's corn-liquor—strong! Got to sneak up on it, 'fore it sneak up on you! Like vodka." Ignoring him, I drank the liquor down in one gulp. He shook his head, dismissing me with a wave of his hand. His friend across the table started snoring, his head thrown back, his mouth wide open, revealing his back gold fillings. He fell forward, pulled back by the man just before his face fell into a pineapple-upside-down cake. I joined the man in a duet of raucous laughter, which combined with the liquor sent me into a spasm of exhausting hiccups.

"Get some ice water," my mentor advised, his face a blur, his words coming from faraway. I got up unsteadily, holding onto the back of the chair, waiting for the room to stop whirling around me like a merry-go-round.

I felt strong hands holding onto me as I waded through a sea of wavy faces to the staircase. I was passed to a feminine shape who climbed with me up the stairs, then walked me down the hall to the children's room, her soft voice murmuring in my ear. She laid me on the bed.

Chapter 3

———◆———

Thunder rolled like the beating of drums. I opened my eyes. The room was black and silent. I lay in bed by myself, fully clothed, my head throbbing, my limbs and lower back on fire. I couldn't remember how I got here, or when. I watched a flash of lightning zip through a patch of sky framed by the window at my side. A fat white moon hung on a canvas of pure black, relieved only by a single pair of stars thrown into the darkness like dice tumbled from an unseen hand.

Zigzags of lightning suddenly formed eerie fluorescent trees all across the sky, followed by a low rumble of thunder. Raindrops splashed loudly on the window, erupting into torrents. I watched the vertical tributary coursing swiftly past the window to the sea of rainwater below. Thunder rattled faintly, barely audible over the rain dancing uproariously on the roof, mounting to a crescendo of exuberant stomping, before gently easing into a steady tapping gait. I lay mesmerized by the voice of the glorious rain, lulling me to dreamless sleep.

The sun's flames seared the sky orange-red, rudely awakening me as they fired through the window. I sat up at the edge of the bed woozy, holding my smarting head and listening to the tub water running. "Courage, my soul," Mama sang triumphantly, "and let us journey on, though the night is dark, and I am far from home—"

I gingerly lifted myself up, and walked haltingly across the floor, every step shooting hot pain through my limbs. A wave of dizziness sent me back to the bed. I sank my face into the cool softness of the pillow, lying on my side to ameliorate the pain in my lower back. Before me the heavens flared red, like a thousand campfires lighting simultaneously.

"Thanks be to God—the morning light appears." I slowly stretched out my legs and arms, breathing slowly, my head aching from last night's whiskey. I needed cool water for my face, but was too weak to get back up.

"Hallelujah-Hal-le-lu-ja-a-ah—"

Goo's soft shoes paddled across the floor. I looked up into her face, glowing beatifically in the bright sunlight. She set the tray she was holding on the end table, the smell of hot soup rising into my nostrils enticingly. She stroked my hot cheek with her cool, soft hand, then wiped my face all over with a wet washcloth. "I heard what happened—Billy and I got into it good this morning. You didn't hear us?"

I shook my head no.

"I told him if he wants to beat someone, it best be that heifer next time—or else!" She sighed. "No more wine for me until Christmas—store bought and one glass! If I'd been awake— Willie, I'm so sorry!" She took my hand and held it in hers, tears in her eyes. I squeezed her hand.

"Goo, I need to tell you—"

"I heard about that, too!"

I was stunned, wondering how she knew about my prayer.

"So tell me—which hurts worse, your head for the whiskey, or the rest of you from Billy?"

So she didn't know about the prayer—she was talking about the drinks. I shamed before her wounded eyes, vowing never to touch liquor again. She laughed. "You remember the time your cousin gave you that cigar? I swear you turned green!"

I laughed weakly, glad to see her smile again. She helped me sit up, and I lay plopped against the pillow, as she fed me the hot soup in spoonfuls, along with some cold juice.

"Kookie came by this morning. I told her you overslept — that's all I told her," she told me, as she tenderly salved the welts on my arms.

I smiled at her gratefully. "Someone was looking out for your Uncle last night. He could be sitting in jail this morning."

She pulled down my trousers and began salving my legs. "And that fool boy — that's all he was, really — someone really looked out for him. I would have bet all my money on him leaving the station!"

I decided to keep the prayer I said for Uncle a precious secret, my earlier attempt at revelation bringing me only trouble. (But despite his spiteful and unfair chastening of me, resulting in prickly red welts I endured for several weeks, Uncle still had not lost his allure to me, and I would obstinately cling to my misguided fascination with his freewheeling self-indulgence and strutting machismo, which my budding self mistook for manhood.)

Mama entered the room, still slowly fastening the top of her dress. Buttons were a menace to her stiff fingers, but she persevered, letting out a heavy sigh as she finished looking in the wall mirror at her handiwork with a satisfied smile. Then she came over and kissed me on the cheek. "Your mother will have you better in no time," she assured me cheerfully. She patted my arm. "Willie, you're young — you'll be runnin' around with that little gal in no time! And Billy's bound to pick up the same card he's dealt out, don't you worry!"

She nodded at me, turning to leave, then turned back around gazing at me intensely. "But you keep praying for Billy, just the same. Nothin' wrong with that! Prayer is the victor—you know it, don't you Willie?" She raised her arms like an arthritic Baptist preacher giving blessing.

I gulped, a chill running through me, to realize her eyes were looking into my soul.

"I'll see you when I get back from church." Grandmother's gold cross gleamed on her black dress as she leaned over to kiss me again.

"There are twelve gates to the city," she sang as she left the room, "my, yes, streets are paved in gold. Yes, Lord, walls are made of jasper—" Her voice faded as she reached the bottom of the steps.

Goo fluffed the pillow up for me, humming the rest of the song Mama began. I settled into the pillow, ready for what-ever the day would bring.

The next week found me still recuperating from Uncle's beating, and it was with great difficulty that I managed to dress myself and walk stiffly to school. I continued to in-wardly burn with resentment every time I saw him, and we encountered each other with mutual silence, one of us leav-ing the room-or-porch as soon as the other appeared.

Living with Mama on 22nd and Grace was brief, when Goo and my father decided to move on to 610 Henry Street, near Belvidere Boulevard. Life on Henry Street turned out to be very rewarding. We shared the house with the owners, the Jacobs, and I became fast friends with Tiny, their son. We explored the city together, enjoying all the hustle and bustle of Broad Street's people-coated sidewalks, where black and white shoppers co-mingled easily despite major stores and restaurants still being segregated. We ran gleefully down the street, past expensive shoe shops and millinery, as well as old imposing movie theatres, and modern drugstores, both providing romantically cozy balconies and booths, perfect for teen-aged trysts, especially on a Saturday night.

But the older boys from our neighborhood would all congregate at the Hippodrome Theatre, located at 528 North Second Street, in Jackson Ward. Another theatre for black moviegoers was the Booker T., at Adam & Broad Street, near the Charles Department Store. Uncle Jack would often take us all out to the movies, picking us up in his brand new Cadillac. (He took us to school every day as well, and we were the envy of our classmates). We children preferred westerns or detective shows, but when sepia star Dorothy Dandridge filled the screen with her beautiful face and form, Uncle Jack would go into a trance, oblivious to soda being spilled on his best pants, or popcorn kernels sailing back and forth over his head as my sisters and I took advantage of his catatonic state, until some matron, not as transfixed by Dorothy, took it upon herself to roughly whack one of us on the head, coupling it with a stern warning to desist from any further horseplay.

On Sundays, Tiny and I would window shop at Thalhimer's and Miller & Rhoads department stores, known throughout Virginia for their beautiful display windows, enchanting both children and adults each Christmastime. After dreaming of all the merchandise we'd buy if we had the money, we'd walk to the State Capitol grounds and feed the birds. In the evening, we'd stop by Planters Peanut Store for sweet treats.

Mrs. Jacobs allowed us to sit on the front porch steps in the evenings and sometimes on Sundays as well. Her yard was a delightful play area, with both a peach and pear tree providing us big luscious fruit in winter and summer. Every evening she would prepare a four- or five-course meal, which would have resulted in a nightly feast, had the helpings been as large as those to which we were accustomed. So we savored many dishes, but none to the point of satiety. Nor did she believe in children eating many sweets, so dessert was only served on special occasions and holidays.

Discipline was doled out by our hostess in the same sufficient measure as mealtime portions. At the time, we felt Mrs. Jacobs often lacked compassion and sensitivity, but with adult hindsight, my memory of her is of a warm but very firm woman, who loved us enough to keep us on the right path, even when it meant taking stern measures whenever we veered off it. This very short lady with a French roll of mixed gray and white hair will always hold a big place in my heart, as will her sister, who closely resembled her in appearance, though their temperaments were complete opposites. We called her sister Aunt Pogy, and we preferred her supervision, as she allowed us to do a lot of things Mrs. Jacobs wouldn't have stood for a minute.

Goo and Mrs. Jacobs were good friends also, and they would often tend us together, laughing and gossiping as they shucked corn or snapped beans on the porch, watching us run and play in the yard. We were forbidden to visit with the children who lived across the alleyway behind us, as both Goo and Mrs. Jacobs felt they were too rough for us to play with out of their sight; but they did allow them to play with us in the front where they could keep a vigilant eye on things. (We were also forbidden to go one block north of where we lived, as Mrs. Jacobs felt it was too dangerous and the residents were most unfriendly). I continued to miss Kookie, and was secretly planning to walk all the way to Southside Richmond to see her one day, a plan that would land me in an interesting adventure later that summer.

But in the meantime, we enjoyed going to Uncle Lee's house after school every afternoon. Uncle lived one block from our current school, Bellevue Elementary, and Aunt Bern would always have homemade cookies and big glasses of milk ready for us. One winter day, Uncle Jack was unable to pick us up from Lee's house, due to a huge snowstorm that paralyzed Richmond for several days. On the second day, we ran out of food, and no one was able to bring us any because of the storm. My cousin Bumpy, who had been at a friend's house in Church Hill when the storm hit, had been so determined to get back home, he got up early that morning and walked all day, arriving at Uncle Lee's very late that afternoon. He brought home some frozen apples that he had found at Eighteenth and Franklin Street Market. We thawed them out over the stove, jumping up and down for joy of having something to eat. Apples were never so tasty as that afternoon in Uncle's warm kitchen, the wind outside moaning as it whipped past the window.

This was to be our only food until Aunt Bern received her paycheck the next day, lavishing us with a bounteous meal, after first teasing our olfactory senses for several hours with mouth watering aromas of roast beef and freshly baked apple pie combining in the air, as all of us cooped-up ravenous youngsters tried to make do with the baked crust sticks sprinkled with sugar and cinnamon she served us while dinner cooked. Uncle Jack joined us in our repast, after which he drove us home. We fell asleep in the backseat, groggy from our gluttonizing.

Goo and Mrs. Jacobs were waiting for us at the door, Goo placing warm wet kisses all over our cold faces while Mrs. Jacobs, usually not physically demonstrative, gave each of us a quick welcoming hug. Then they took us upstairs for what was a favorite evening ritual of mine. Several of my sisters and I would climb into the big 1920s bathtub, resting on four porcelain paws, fashionable at that time. Then Goo and Mrs. Jacobs would bathe us in the tub with very soapy water and sponges, which was a fun novelty for us, as we had always used washcloths. They would scrub us so hard getting us clean we sometimes thought our skin would come off, but they instilled in me a love of cleanliness which served me well when I later joined the Air Force, with its strictly enforced regulations concerning clean and orderly quarters. But for now, I thoroughly enjoyed running my hands through the soapy water, making large ripples while my sisters squealed in delight. We climbed into bed clean as a whistle and elated to be back home.

It was a week before Memorial Day. For weeks, spring and summer had vigorously jostled each other in a topsy-turvy contention of warm muggy afternoons toppled by a long fit of pounding evening rainstorms, till at last, searing hot summer emerged victorious, haughtily covering the air with a veil of sticky humidity. Only intermittently had each tantalizingly warm spring day settled down comfortably in the city of Richmond, inviting you to bask in her brief glory by stirring the heady scents of blossoming flowers with a meandering, refreshingly cool breeze, gently rippling the fresh green grass, the soft sunlight a perfect backdrop for a shimmering sea of color. There had been about a week of such glory days in early May. Then they were abruptly gone.

Fiery sunlight flashed through the blinds, rudely rousing me from a blissful dream, composed of various excursions with Kookie—we walked by the pond feeding the ducks, then we strolled down a secluded path between rows of elm trees, squirrels swiftly scampering up the trunks and perching on limbs as we approached. Then she took my hand, and I briefly thrilled at the touch of her warm softness, vanishing abruptly as I opened my eyes, watching my own image in the dresser mirror next to our bed, lines of light spreading across my now despondent face.

My sisters were already up and about their chores, as it was Saturday and "no one could have any fun till chores were done," as Goo would say. Cranky due to my faded reverie of Kookie, seemingly lost to me now, my irritation increased at having overslept, as now I would be behind on my chores. I decided to bribe one of my sisters into doing my share—I could sometimes do this with an amount of quarters, or I would sometimes offer to bake a batch of chocolate chip cookies for them later in the week, if they could help me out on Saturday morning. Since I was the better cook, this ploy usually worked, provided it was Goo's day to be at the beauty parlor (she worked every other Saturday) and Mrs. Jacobs was distracted with Mrs. Henry, (a neighbor who would often visit in the morning, drinking coffee, eating 2 or 3 slices of Mrs. Jacobs' homemade coffee cakes, adding pounds to her already more than ample girth!) Otherwise, if either or both were present and alert, neither would countenance this sibling finagling and I wouldn't get out to play until mid-afternoon.

I threw back the covers and lay on my back a moment in the middle of the bed, my flesh covered with sweat in the already sizzling air. Birds chattered fiercely, approaching a melody with their trumpeting trills, as an orange-red sun languidly climbed the azure sky. One little bird made a low "woo-whoo" sound, a lonely cry in the midst of his gregarious gurgling neighbors.

I rolled over on my side, then lowered my squat legs to the floor, washing up quickly in the bathroom sink before descending to the kitchen to discover my fate. I reached the bottom of the stairs, happily listening to Mrs. Henry's piercing laughter, normally annoying. I proceeded to the hall leading to the kitchen, peeping in at the two women, breathing a sigh of relief at Goo's absence from her favorite chair, the one closest to the window. I listened a minute as they animatedly discussed some neighborhood Lothario, caught sneaking out the window by an unexpectedly home-early husband, who doused him with the garden hose, then sicked his German shepherd on his retreating form. The young man climbed over the fence at breakneck speed, barely escaping the canine teeth snapping at his heels.

At the end of this sordid tale, Mrs. Jacobs poured more coffee and sliced more cake, as they ate between anecdotes. I slipped back down the hall unheeded by the mirthful duo, hurriedly looking for one of my sisters so we could close a deal. I found Jamie dusting Goo's dresser top, and immediately proposed a trade-off of her cleaning and dusting upstairs in exchange for my famous chocolate chip cookies. She agreed, but made an additional claim for one dollar worth of quarters. I hesitated, but since she had me over the proverbial barrel, I acquiesced.

So she went down the hall and I quietly opened the front door, sinking into my rocker contentedly. Jamie had agreed to bring me an iced tea from the kitchen, so I watched our neighbors working or relaxing in their yards while I waited. A boy I knew skated down the sidewalk, waving deftly, skirting a mother walking her toddler, followed at some length by a man with a sheep dog, who when he saw me bounded away from his owner, down our sidewalk and onto the porch, ardently licking my face, his smelly mangy hair sickening me. "Get away from me! Go on!" I pushed her away roughly.

"Sino, come here, c'mon here, girl!" Her owner had come halfway up the walk and was calling a stubborn Sino as Jamie appeared with my iced tea. The dog settled at my feet, her long tongue protruding as she panted heavily in the swelling heat. Jamie whacked her hard on the back as she handed me my tea, and she whimpered and trotted off to her owner, indifferently watching our coarse treatment of his none-too-well taken-care-of pet. They continued up the sidewalk, Sino, who apparently liked children, approaching another boy who knelt down, rubbing her head and good-naturedly receiving wet licks all over his little face.

Jamie sat down for a moment in Goo's big rocker, lifting her head in matronly imitation, surveying the yard with the prim expression of a head librarian. She would frequently put on grownup airs like this, which amused me to no end, and I chuckled softly as I sipped my tea.

She whirled around and shot me a look. "What's so funny?"

"Nothing," I lied.

She clicked her tongue, a sound she made when disgusted or in disbelief. "Mrs. Jacobs' tulips sure are pretty." Mrs. Jacobs had planted a small circle of red tulips all around her birch tree, and they swayed in the warm breeze, creating a startling contrast with the stark white bark of the tree, like the parted glistening lips of a big cherry-red mouth revealing even white teeth.

"Yeah," I jeered, still miffed about the quarters she demanded, "too bad Barry doesn't think the same about you." (I knew this would rile her. She had a crush on a boy in our class, who fended off all her fervent glances with an averted eye.) As expected, she bristled.

"Boy, you're too silly, when I get your age, I'm not gonna be near as babified." She crossed her arms and tilted her head further back.

"Miss Nose-in-the-Air, you smell somethin' bad?" I countered. "Must have forgot to wash your armpits again, huh?"

With that, she kicked me on the shin, and dashed back through the door, knowing I couldn't retaliate, as any commotion would draw Mrs. Jacob's unwanted attention. "I'll get you later, Miss Hoity-Toity," I mumbled to myself.

Just then Carol Hinley, one of Uncle Billy's old flames,

pulled up in her green Chevrolet, primping in her rearview mirror, running her finger lightly through her poodle hairdo, then prissing up to the porch in search of Uncle, knowing he often came by on Saturdays. Uncle had stopped seeing her, as he "didn't like being gum-shoed by some female everywhere I go," as he told it. Then about a month ago, she was back on the scene, although at this time the number one position in Uncle's hit parade of dalliances now belonged to Karla Mason.

She gave me a luminous smile as she ascended the porch steps in spectator pumps, admittedly very attractive in her white sleeveless blouse—unbuttoned at the top to form a tastefully provocative low V—and a tight navy blue skirt. She eased into Goo's rocker, laying her red-nailed hand on my shoulder, her perfume a little too pungent in the thick hot air. "How have you been, Willie? No doubt, you're still cranking out those As?"

"Oh, yes ma'am." I gave her what I though was my most winsome smile. Though she was phony and snooty, I was determined to be pleasant, as I had formulated an idea and would need her help. I continued smiling, dreading she would ask for a glass of iced tea, which would send me to the kitchen and ruin everything. She sat daintily in the rocker, continuing to smooth her coiffure with her hand.

C'mon—ask me if he's here, I thought, rocking slowly and emulating Jamie's earlier nonchalant gaze over the yard. On cue, she asked me Uncle's whereabouts. I mentioned one of his Southside hangouts, implying he had just headed there from our house. She took the bait, quickly taking out her compact and dabbing at her pretty face, then adding another coat of lipstick to her already-painted red lips. "He was alone, wasn't he?" she asked casually as she outlined her lips in the mirror.

"He was alone when he left," I proffered, mock-innocently, "but from what I hear, he won't be alone for long!"

She lowered her lipstick, her large eyes widening. "Really? And just what did you hear Willie?" she asked sweetly, encircling me with her arm. I leaned over towards her confidentially, feeding her hopes with an artful insinuation. "One evening, Uncle was on the porch talking with my mother. I was in the yard playing, and no one thought I was paying any attention." I paused for dramatic effect—Carol sat on the edge of Goo's rocker, her hungry ear devouring every morsel served up from my lying lips. I heard him say, "'Got that diamond lined up—and the last payment on the ring will be in June. Yeah, sis,' he said, 'that's when I'm gonna get that ring—in June!'"

"And did he say who the ring was for?" she asked breathlessly.

"For his greatest love!"

She laid her hand on her breast in blissful disbelief. "For his greatest love," she murmured, closing her eyes. Actually it wasn't a boldfaced lie, just a partial revelation of facts. Uncle did have a ring in lay-away that he had mentioned would be paid up for in June—a man's diamond ring, for himself, truly his greatest love. So it wasn't my fault that Carol had drawn a totally fanciful tableau—or so I convinced myself, temporarily assuaging my guilt for what I know in my nether regions was a humongous fib.

And since my plan involved my own "love" Kookie, I felt completely justified in fanning this burned-out flame. There was a risk involved—once she slipped this exchange to Uncle, I might end up with yet another beating. But I believed that I could convince him she'd misunderstood what I said, since he had mentioned the ring in front of me. Besides, I was still angry with him and felt no compunction at saddling him with Carol's misguided amorous advances. Actually, I was relishing the vision of his ducking and dodging all over town.

As she rose to leave, I confidently made my pitch. "Miss Carol, I wanted to go see an old friend of mine today. Mother said it was all right. Uncle Billy was supposed to take me, but I overslept and hadn't finished my chores yet when he came over—and, well, you know Uncle he didn't want to wait, though I was finished not five minutes after he left." I let out a pitiable sigh.

"Is your Uncle Jack picking you up later?" I nodded, glad she was familiar enough with family routine to render my tale feasible.

"Well, go tell your mother we're leaving. I'll be in the car."

"Yes Ma'am!"

I opened the front door quietly and crossed through the front room to the closet, peeping out and making sure Mrs. Henry didn't decide to leave right now. I could still hear her conversing with Mrs. Jacobs in the kitchen. After an interminably long thirty seconds, I noiselessly slipped back out the door, making a big to-do of waving as I closed it, as if to my approving mother. I scampered down the walk, my heart beating loudly in my chest. Carol opened the car door for me, and I plopped down onto the front seat, dreading the sudden appearance of some adult thus far oblivious to my crime. Carol put her sunglasses on, and away we went, me heaving a big sigh of relief at having made it out of the yard undetected. My scheme was running smoothly and perfectly—but it was about to crash.

Carol drove very sedately, and we ambled down the street too slowly for my purposes. I cast a nervous eye at our front door, but no one appeared. She turned on the car radio, and as

"Raunchy" played softly, we paced along street after street, barely stirring up a breeze through the open windows.

I wiped the sweat pouring down my face with my hands, as Carol daintily dabbed at her face with a silk handkerchief, her smooth brown skin covered by only a thin veil of perspiration. We had reached the vicinity of Oregon Hill, and suddenly began speeding past rows of shabby shot-gun houses cramped together among disheveled yards, cluttered with worn-out tires, broken down cars, and barefoot white children running through the stubby grass.

We turned, and began going down Lakeview Avenue, and I was relieved to see black residents appearing again. (Whites in the Oregon Hill area and environs were very territorial and didn't like blacks to come through their area. I had heard many stories from boys who had been jumped trying to pass through these areas on foot. One boy had been waylaid several times as he tried to pass through to Lee Bridge, surprising his attackers the next time they accosted him by inflicting swift and furious switchblade cuts on their much larger frames, leaving them bleeding and crumpled in pain next to the bushes behind which they had hidden as he scrambled past them to the bridge. The story of this pint-size bluffer, outnumbered and outsized, luring his stronger foes to defeat with a show of timidity, taught me a valuable lesson about overconfidence: whoever carried it into the fight will be carried out!)

But my relief at being on Lakeview was short-lived. Several blocks down on the right I saw it. I tried to distract her, pointing out some amply beautiful red rose bushes in the yard across the street. She looked, and for one foolish moment I actually thought we were going to make it past Uncle's Oldsmobile parked in front of Karla's small two-story house. (Oh, why didn't I remember she lived on Lakeview?)

Carol jerked the car over abruptly, pulling in behind Uncle's car, her face turned ashen as she turned off the motor.

"Jive two-timer!" She added some choicer names, all her sedateness consumed in her fury. "If he thinks I'm marrying him after he's had coochie with that hoochie Karla—"

This was not going well. She was already getting out of the car, so I had to get out of here fast before Uncle got hold of me. No sooner had she reached the fence gate than I high-tailed it up the street, spying her still stepping quickly up the walk as I ran around the corner. Unfortunately, I was right back in the white residential section we had just passed through, so I sped up even more, looking down the street at a group of children playing in the street, watched their none-too-friendly looking t-shirted fathers standing by their pickup trucks and smoking cigarettes, one man spitting his chewed tobacco juice into the grass.

I ran back to the corner undetected, deciding to cut through the alley. (Had I left my stubborn streak at home, home is where I would have gone, but I carried it with me, persevering on my ill-advised mission to cross Lee Bridge and surprise Kookie.) Anticipating the heavenly taste of Mrs. Winston's hot buttered dinner rolls, I ran faster and faster down the deserted alleyway—and then I froze, looking dead into a pair of glowering canine eyes.

The dog had sprung forward from the next yard on the right running the length of his chain, then posting himself protectively at the very edge of the yard. I stood stock-still, averting my eyes from those of the Doberman, who had moved several feet down now, snarling and showing his sharp white teeth. Then he quieted, just standing there in the grass daring me to pass.

The alley was rather narrow, but I gauged he could reach me if I slipped by on the other side, so I slowly traversed the rim of several yards to the left. I looked straight ahead, but kept my corner eye on the dog, who began barking fiercely. My fear turned to anger as I heard a back screen door open, the dog continuing to yelp angrily in an ironic attempt to sic his owner on me. I looked around for anything I could use as a weapon, should I have to defend myself, quickly grabbing a large rock, then running on towards the corner.

As I neared Idlewood Avenue, I passed an ancient white woman taking out her garbage, watching me impassively. Her skin was as white as unused paper, drifting down her neck in drooping folds, wrinkling around her bulbous eyes, as blue as the pebble Kookie gave me. She placed the lid back on the rusty can and walked stooping back to her house, her frayed blue bathrobe swallowing her tiny frame.

I turned the corner onto Belvidere, stopping to catch my breath, dripping with sweat, bending over and taking large gulps of humid air. The sky was ablaze with an orange sun at its zenith. I passed a succession of businesses interspersed with old frame houses. In front of a busy service station, several boys stood by a Coke machine, raising the ice-cold bottles to their lips. I checked my pockets for change but they were empty.

I skirted a pile of garbage strewn across the sidewalk, sickening from its putrid odor rising in the cloying heat. A herd of sleek, shiny cars and rickety trucks advanced past me, trailing clouds of charcoal grey smoke ascending in the air. As they dispersed, Spring Street Penitentiary came into view, so I know I was only four or five blocks from the Bridge. I thought of one of Uncle's friends, Joe "Scrappy" Howard, who was living behind those walls now. He'd gotten into a fight over a poker game, a fight that turned deadly for the other man. But he'd only gotten a year for his crime; had he killed a white man, he'd have gotten life or the chair. Joe had family already residing there when he arrived, a young cousin from Waynesboro, Virginia accused of raping an elderly white women and now serving a life sentence.

I averted my eyes from the prison and looked towards two older black men fishing off Lee Bridge in the distance. Traffic was sparse for this time of day, and as I neared the bridge, their mellow laughter spilled out into the unusual quiet, like a refreshing drizzle of raindrops cooling the oppressive air. As I reached the men, one of them picked up a large thermos and poured water into a plastic cup, which he handed to the other man. I stood before the man with the thermos, looking up at him imploringly as he poured water for himself. He looked down at me, holding the blue plastic cup of water in one hand, his other hand still holding his fishing pole, his black face glistening with sweat under a shock of white hair, his wide-brimmed straw hat pushed back on his egg-shaped head. He handed me the cup, and I drank the cold water down in huge gulps. "More?"

I nodded, and he poured me another cup. This time, I drank more slowly, standing beside the two men, looking down into the river, wishing I were as patient as these men resting in peaceful alertness, ready to wait all afternoon for one bite on the line. I watched their faraway eyes as they stared into the water, appearing to see all kinds of thing I couldn't yet.

"Terrance!" A girl in a plain white cotton dress walked wearily on the bridge, calling to a small shirtless boy running way ahead of her. "Terrance, come back here!" she shouted exasperatedly at her charge, who ignored her, scampering excitedly towards our trio. Lickety-split, he was standing next to me, jumping up and down excitedly as he peered down into the water. He grinned at me, his chubby cheeks poking out like a beaver's, his buckteeth sticking out over his lower lip. But his bright brown eyes lit up his coffee-colored face and I smiled back at him, glad for his company, as we jumped up and down together.

"Stop that, boy!" the other man fussed. He hadn't spoken to or looked at us and was obviously grouchier than his companion. We quit jumping, giggling to ourselves at his crabbiness.

"Chill out, Garvy! What's the problem?" the other fisherman queried. Garvy just scowled. My new cohort then picked up a rock, throwing it into the water with gusto. It hit the water with a loud splash, rippling the surface just on the other side of the more genial man's line.

"I told you two devils to keep still! Don't care if you hear the Judgment Day horn—not a peep!"

"Your drawers too tight today? What's got your hide, you old goat?"

"They're scarin' the fish off! 'Sides, you're older than me, you long-toothed buzzard!"

"Fish? What fish? We've been here since early this morning, and nothin's bitin' but your tongue!" By this time, the older girl had caught up with Terrance, scolding him soundly as the men continued to bicker. A strong facial resemblance indicated they were brother and sister. She was a pretty girl, but her eyes registered a resignation incongruous with her youth. She grabbed his hand, pulling him roughly along behind her as they continued over the bridge. He turned and looked at me dolefully for a few seconds before snapping his head back around, prying loose from his sister's grip, scampering off ahead of her as lively as a June bug. "Terrance, come back here!" she shouted, and off they went in their sibling rivalry. I shook my head, laughing at my departing chum's vivacious tenacity.

The men had settled back down into a comfortable silence, so I went my way after drinking one last cup of water. Traffic was picking up, and irate motorists were blowing their horns at a slowpoke in a Green Buick, an elderly man in a white linen suit, moseying ahead, nonplussed by all the commotion and cussing, his captive procession inching behind him like a pack of turtles.

It wasn't until we were two blocks down Cowardin that the bottleneck of traffic began to flow again. At last I turned onto Hull Street, my heart pounding in anticipation of nearing 10th Street and the Winstons' house. Black and white shoppers milled around the sidewalks together, though the restaurants were segregated. A husky white vendor sat at his table holding up some dangly, jingly glass beads to catch my eye. There were cases of cheap watches and rings laid out for inspection, along with some ladies' broaches, none of which were particularly unique or appealing. I would have loved to have bought a ring for Kookie, had I brought some of my mayonnaise-jar quarters.

A whiff of warm chocolate drew me to the next vendor, a plump red-headed lady who gestured toward her candy with a graceful flourish of her chubby hand, its porcelain smoothness marred by large liver spots. Moist chocolate fudge squares gleamed on strips of wax paper centered between paper cups of lemonade. The lady crossed her plump arms over her red- checkered apron, smiling as I stared wistfully at the candy and cold drink. I looked up into her kind green eyes. "Do you give samples?" I asked boldly, trying my best to look pitiful.

The lady pursed her lips. "Well," she was already picking up one of the thick chocolate squares, "you just be sure to tell all your friends how delicious my fudge is." She handed me the candy. "Guess it pays to spread the word, so tell them about my fresh lemonade as well." She handed me a cup, pushing her unruly red hair behind her ears.

"Yes ma'am, I sure will. Thank you, ma'am!" I responded enthusiastically, already walking away, sinking my teeth into the slightly warm fudge, washing it down with the cup of tart lemonade. I began to believe my luck was changing for the better as I ambled downhill, only a few blocks away from 10th Street. I peeped into a furniture store window, admiring a green velvet sofa, flanked by cherry wood tables, atop of each a beautiful Tiffany lamp, their jewel colors glowing. I pressed my head against the glass, surveying all the exquisite chairs and rugs, my heart beating furiously as a large male hand clamped down on my shoulder, the index finger sporting a familiar square turquoise ring. I dropped my cup as he whirled me around, staring down at his spit-polished shoes till he lifted my face up with his hand. I looked into Uncle's eyes resignedly, wondering if my beating would occur on the sidewalk or someplace else. I waited as he looked over me impassively, his arms folded.

"I understand I'm gonna be jumping the broom." He examined his manicured nails, letting me sweat a few more minutes. "You better run along to the Winstons. Don't forget to call Jack to pick you up later." He stuck out his arm motioning me up the sidewalk. "Well, go on!"

I knew better than to fall for this, so I started walking ahead of him to the car, halfway expecting to be grabbed and pulverized on the way. Karla sat in the front seat sipping a soda. I had seen her numerous times before and knew she was extremely quiet, so I got into the back seat without speaking, figuring since Uncle had his lady with him, I'd catch whatever licks were coming later.

He got in, and we started down Hull Street. "We have to let Willie out at 10th, don't we?" he continued to needle, looking at me in the rearview mirror to see my reaction, but I made none, glancing out the window at the shoppers, as Uncle unexpectedly pulled the car over to the curb and parked again. Uh-oh—he's going to take me into the alley. I thought about running down Hull and getting away, but that would just postpone the inevitable, so I decided to get it all over with, slowly getting out of the back as Uncle exited the front. "You're coming, too?" I shrugged my shoulders. "Okay—c'mon." Reckoning him to be toying with me further, I started towards the alleyway. "Where are you going?" He motioned me back, leaning over to talk to Karla. "I'm going in here to get us some sandwiches. Believe it or not, their turkey's better than Gregory's—Gregory's getting thin on those slices—got to do better than that. C'mon, Willie."

We walked down to 12th and Hull and entered the Lighthouse Restaurant, an appropriate name for this white establishment that didn't allow black customers to eat at the tables or sit at the counter, where they placed their orders. We walked back to the counter, unheeded by the crowd of shoppers having their lunch. A large family of diners was getting up from their stools as Uncle placed the order for our food. We continued standing, though all the counter seats were now empty. I wished we had waited and gone to Gregory's, even if the turkey portions weren't as generous. I really felt uneasy being around so many whites who made it known that they didn't care for black people, although as long as you followed expected protocol, the diners ignored you, and usually you could take your food and leave without incident. Besides, I was still anxious about where and when I would be getting my beating.

So we waited in silence, Uncle standing with his hands in his blue pants pockets, the smell of good home-cooked food making me ravenous as I restlessly drummed my fingers on the countertop. A ceiling fan sluggishly stirred up the torrid air, barely cooling it. Out of the corner of my eye, I saw a lady in a sleeveless pink dress approach the counter, sitting a few stools down from where we were standing. "Whew, it's hot down here," she said in a funny accent, tossing her canary yellow hair as she sat looking at a lunch menu lying open on the counter.

Was she talking to us? The lady who took our order was still in the back, and no other diners had come over yet. She never looked at us, nor did Uncle look at her. "I'm from Vermont," she continued softly, lifting her eyes ever so slightly away from the menu and onto Uncle's face. "There's nothing so beautiful as snow-covered mountains."

Uncle stiffened, his face turning to granite. I didn't understand what she was talking about, but I knew Uncle didn't like it one bit. The other lady came back out and took the blonde woman's order, quickly disappearing again into the kitchen. Uncle took out his wallet, retrieving the money for our sandwiches. I waited nervously in the familiar quietness that preceded the potential breaking out of one his numerous inner storms. Go away, lady, just go away, I silently demanded. Whatever's going on, you're irritating Uncle, and I'll be the one catching extra wallops on my backside!

Then she got out a piece of paper from her purse, writing something down, then folding it into a small square and laying it in the ashtray placed between us on the counter. Just for that moment, Uncle turned his face towards her. He flicked her away with his eyes, like so much lint from his lapel. Oblivious to his unspoken dismissal of her, she pushed the ashtray closer to him, still looking down at the much-perused menu, gently patting her face with a white linen handkerchief. Uncle pushed the ashtray back towards her. "I don't like snow," he said quietly but evenly, staring ahead blankly, slipping his wallet back into his pocket. The blonde lady's face turned red.

"Did you say something?" The other lady had returned with our food and sodas.

"I was just telling my nephew that I don't like snow."

"Oh. Here you are, Virginia." She handed the blonde woman her sandwich. "Are you alright, Ginny?"

"I'm fine—just flushed from this heat. Thanks." She turned and walked quickly away, sheepishly slipping out the door. Uncle paid for our food and we left.

"Uncle," I asked as soon as we were outside, "how come you told that lady you don't like snow?" He had always joined in when we boys threw snowballs at each other, and had helped Jamie and me build a snowman last winter. His deep baritone laughter reassured me that the rising swell of his anger had subsided—for now, anyway. "I like snow-covered mountains just fine, Willie. As long as they're in Vermont and I don't have to climb!" Puzzled by his mysterious joke, I didn't want to mess up his sudden affability by forcing the issue, so I settled into the back seat, sinking my teeth into the thick turkey sandwich, swigging my grape soda, as Uncle pulled Karla closer. "Come here, brown sugar," he whispered loudly, kissing her full on the lips. "What we need now is some strawberry ice cream, right, Willie?"

I nodded as Karla eased even closer to Uncle, who made a right turn at 11th Street, circling back to Hull in a horseshoe configuration of turns. Ironically, I had come within one block of my destination and my disappointment started to swell, diminishing my enjoyment of the succulent turkey.

Uncle parked across from Gregory's, which was at 19th and Hull. The restaurant was located on the first level of a two-story building, along with a pool hall and barbershop (later turned into a beauty salon). On the second level was Gregory's Ballroom, where Uncle and his latest lady would go on Saturday nights for drinks and dancing. We got out and crossed the street, Uncle mingling with the male congregation near the entrance, gesticulating and whistling at various attractive young ladies coming into Gregory's. Some of the men shot sidelong glances at Karla, and no doubt if Uncle hadn't been there, this pack of wolves would have encircled her by now.

We stood waiting for Uncle, as male motorists honked their horns, calling sundry entreaties to Karla out their car windows. I stood next to her sipping my soda, closing my eyes, and as Uncle bantered with his friends, I listened—really listened for the first time in my life—to the soul-sustaining sound of black men, sharing blessedly free camaraderie, their reverberating voices merging con brio into one steady rhythmic flow of life, washing over me in the enervating heat.

I opened my eyes as Uncle opened the door, motioning Karla and me into Gregory's, which was crowded with families, lovers, and friends communing raucously, the first notes of "Earth Angel" barely audible, playing on the jukebox. Uncle glad-handed his way to a back booth, sitting down long enough to place our order, then getting up again to work the room, moving from booth to table, flirting with the women, jabbering with the men, while Karla and I ate our ice cream in silence.

I glanced at her smooth brown skin, looking for signs of bruising, wondering if Carol had inflicted any injuries before Uncle could step in. But I knew that Karla was above entering the fray, leaving it to Uncle to dispose of her contender either by bodily eviction, or, more likely, by generously pouring out a concoction of lies, excuses, and apologies for Carol to imbibe, designed to send her floating back to her car, intoxicated with the heady brew. This sometimes worked for Uncle when he was in some of his self-produced jams, and since Karla seemed content and feeling no pain, I concluded it had worked this time also. Yet I suspected Uncle best not push his luck with Carol, whose previously hidden temper had appeared to match his own today.

His ice cream was beginning to melt around the edges, and as I saw no need for one of my favorite desserts to go to waste, I slid the bowl over in front of me, gobbling large mouthfuls that chilled my teeth till they ached. Karla applied a fresh layer of red lipstick to her mouth, drawing glances from a group of fellows at a nearby table, noting her escort's protracted absence. Apparently, Uncle had spied their interest as well, finally manifesting his presence at our booth, motioning for us to leave and making no comment about the two empty bowls in front of me.

We passed over Lee Bridge in a steadily growing line of traffic. The two fishermen had gone, replaced by a young couple holding hands, peering dreamily into the water. Uncle had turned quiet, listening to some jazz on the radio, Karla's head resting on his shoulder. I became apprehensive again, wondering if we'd be making any stops on the way home, stops ending with my naked backside smarting from Uncle's belt.

We arrived back at Karla's house and I ran up the walk ahead of them, badly in need of going to the bathroom before I wet my pants. "You pee on Karla's rug—!" Uncle warned me sternly. "It's to the left."

I ran through the living room and entered the most beautiful bathroom I'd ever seen, with lush green plants in the corners and a thick immaculately clean white rug. I flipped on the switch, and pink light bulbs glowed all around the huge vanity mirror. Both the sink and tub had gold fixtures. I decided as I relieved myself that Karla was rich, and that maybe that's why Uncle liked her best. As I washed my hands,

I watched my reflection in the aura of pink light, thinking it made me look spooky, planning to tell Goo we should have pink lights all over the house.

I crept down the hallway, hoping to surreptitiously take a self-guided tour of this elegant house while Karla and Uncle smooched, nestled into the beige Queen Anne-style sofa like turtle doves in the sand, enjoying the darkness provided by damask drapes. Plush Persian rugs covered the highly polished floors.

Sneaking further down the hall, I entered the dining room, where a long mahogany table was set for four. I tiptoed over and peeked at the gold-rimmed plates, painted with pink and purple flowers. I picked up one of the gold spoons, something I'd never seen before.

"You planning to stay for dinner?" Uncle came up beside me, taking the spoon and carefully wiping off any prints with his pocket-handkerchief before setting it back on the table. "C'mon, time to go home."

We left Karla standing between two matching end tables in the front hall, a blue Wedgwood plate on one, a pink-flowered Oriental vase on the other. Uncle kissed her lightly on the cheek as we left.

We drove home in silence, not even the radio on. Anticipating that my thrashing was imminent, I attempted to stall, making small talk, hoping to pique his amusement, in a last-ditch effort to escape or at least mitigate my punishment.

"Miss Karla's rich, isn't she?" He ignored me. "She sure likes pink, doesn't she?" He turned into the parking lot of a diner, parking at the edge by some shrubbery. A few cars were parked near the diner, but no one was around. I waited, preparing myself for the worst.

"We're not gonna try to run away to the Winstons again, are we?" he asked quietly. I shook my head no, disturbed by his use of the word "we," which he often used before disciplining us.

"And we're not going to stick- our- nose-," he emphatically pronounced each word, roughly grabbing my nostrils and pinching them together, "in grownups' business—especially this grownup—right?" I nodded, my nose being twisted in his powerful grip.

With that, he started up the car and drove me home. Goo and Mrs. Jacobs were sitting on the porch when we pulled up. I dreaded Goo's reaction to my escapade, but surprisingly, Uncle stayed in the car advising me to tell her he had come by unexpectedly to treat me to lunch, as he sometimes would do.

I climbed the steps, relieved, promising myself falsely that I would never pull such a stunt again, sinking wearily into my rocker between Goo and Mrs. Jacobs, shaking my head at my erratic Uncle, who sped away, waving to us as he shot by. (I never did get to see Kookie again, but new loves were to beckon me shortly.)

It wasn't long after this incident that I broke this selfward vow never to run away or be disobedient again. One summer day, after visiting relatives in Church Hill with my two sisters, I persuaded them to walk all the way home to Henry Street, instead of taking the bus as planned. They didn't believe I knew the way home, and I took it as a personal challenge to show them that I did. I was vindicated, as we walked all the way home without getting lost. However, when Goo found out what we'd done, we each received a sound beating.

Another time, I decided to walk from Henry to Leigh Street to Uncle Champ's home on Chicago Avenue, a reckless trek, since I had only been there once in my young life. So I amazed myself by arriving there without getting lost one time. I left our house, walked one block to Belvidere, and then began walking towards Southside. I passed the War Memorial which I knew was on the way to Manchester Bridge, so I kept going in that direction, crossing the bridge and continuing to walk till I reached Chicago Avenue, turning right and heading west. I couldn't remember the exact address, but I did remember that it was a large white house with a fence, located in the 2700 block, and just such a house appeared on the next corner.

I ran up the walk and rang the doorbell excitedly. Aunt Molly opened the door, surprised to see me and wanting to know what in the world I was doing there without Goo. She was unable to get a clear answer out of me, so she handed me over to Uncle Champ, who gently pried the information out of me.

They decided to let me spend the night. After Aunt Molly showered me, she fed me a hot meal, then dressed me in a pair of my cousin's pajamas, which were too big, the sleeves hanging down over my hands, the pants drooping down my little legs in large folds. We laughed at my reflection in the mirror, and I played like I was a ghost, holding up my arms and hiding my head in the white pajama top, imitating a headless phantom. Then Aunt Molly kissed me on the cheek and tucked me in. I fell asleep instantly, tired from my imprudent journey. While I slept, she called a distraught Goo and informed her of her wayward son's whereabouts.

The next day, Goo got Uncle Jack to drive her to Champ's to pick me up and carry me home, where Uncle paddled my bottom long and hard. But running away was becoming an obsessive habit for me, despite the escalating chastisement I was receiving. Three months later, I ran away for the last time, leaving our house on a snowy day, this time with the intent of leaving the city of Richmond. I was tired of getting beaten, yet I couldn't seem to rein in my compulsion to wander, so I decided I'd hop a train and go stay with Aunt Florence in Philadelphia. They say she lived in a brand new house with a swimming pool—and best of all, I'd have my own room!

So I went to Broad Street and began walking west, going as far as Willow Lawn Shopping Center, where I went inside Woolsworth's, going back to the lunch counter where I could order a cup of hot chocolate to go (I had brought some quarters this time). Low and behold, Uncle Tom was shopping at the store, and saw me as I headed down the aisle to the back. Knowing full well Goo would never allow me to walk up there by myself—especially in the snow—he gruffly escorted me out to his car and drove me home.

Worse, Uncle Jack was there when we arrived, and judging that the floggings I'd been receiving were evidently not severe enough, he whipped me but good. I lay between his legs, my posterior in an upright position, pleading with him not to hit me anymore. My hard head was literally making for a soft and very sore behind. In retrospect, I believe I intuited I was born to take a journey, and in my youthful exuberance was anxious to get started. But I didn't know yet that the inception of every journey is preparation, and this was its season. Uncle's lashing wore down my resistance and I settled down into my proper seasoning, actually looking forward to returning to school as autumn steadily approached.

Chapter 4

A
nd so Indian summer continued to pass softly through the city, spreading her warm ephemeral glow over the first movements of harvest, then gliding away softly one chilly morning when autumn suddenly stepped back out, taking up the trek of her softer sister in a frisky romp, seducing young and old to join her exuberant revelry. We were spun in a whirl of dazzling sensual delights, relishing the tricks being played on us by our capricious companion: first abruptly frosting the air, then sweetening and spicing its invigorating briskness with scents of apple and pumpkin, then turning around and setting the trees on fire with explosive flames of red, orange, and yellow. We were heady, giddy in a dance of halcyon days as crisp as the leaves crunching under our shoes as we scampered down sidewalks after school, jumping in piles of leaves, grabbing apples from neighbors' trees, savoring hot chocolate and ginger cookies in kitchens bustling with preparations for the coming holidays.

But more than the leaves were being swept away that fall. Slowly, imperceptibly, the wind began to change direction in the Old Dominion, relentlessly blowing away the last vestiges of the Old South that clung to her rotting trunk like dry brittle leaves hanging stubbornly but futilely onto a tree limb whipped by a late autumn storm. It would be a storm of long duration, steady but furious, just beginning to rise this joyous fall, the fall my Uncle Lee found a new home, a move which would eventually lead me into the peaceful eye of that brewing storm.

Uncle Lee was a brick mason, discharged from the Army, and though they say he was good enough to play major league ball, he opted to play on the community baseball team instead, so that he could remain home with his family, supporting them and my grandmother as well. He was the first to leave our large household, moving to Marshall Street between 21st and 22nd streets. This was the area of Richmond known as Church Hill, a beautiful old section which was so named as it was dotted with myriad churches of various denominations, dating back to the days when Richmond's prominent white citizens strolled its cobblestone streets. One of these citizens, Patrick Henry, made his famous "Give me liberty or give me death" speech, delivered at St. John's Church on East Broad Street.

Of course, this liberty was not extended to the slaves still being held in bondage at the time, the descendants of whom settled into various enclaves around the city, such as the Navy Hill area, Fulton, and the royal crown of black Richmond's rulership, Jackson Ward, resplendent with architectural delights—townhouses renowned for their ornamental ironwork, imposing brick churches towering towards heaven in simple stalwart beauty. Regal Jackson Ward bustled with commerce during the day, lighted with celebration during the night, as banks and insurance companies closed for the evening and her streets filled with black patrons streaming to restaurants, theaters, and nightclubs.

But as droves of whites scurried to the suburbs in the postwar boom, neighborhoods began switching hues along with the leaves of the magnificent old maples lining their tranquil shady avenues. Returning black soldiers and their families filtered through the screens of these segregated areas, increasing in parallel number to that of the departing whites, until whole communities were switched in a racial shell game, in which realtors fed fear for profit, although now, ironically, as white suburbanites, with the clearer vision of hindsight, buy back their grandparents' and great-grandparents' houses for renovation).

Uncle Lee—and later our family—formed the latter part of this initial trickle of black residents into white Church Hill. As we were accustomed to living in a predominately black area, we marveled at the idea of Uncle Lee and his immediate family of four living in an integrated neighborhood. Other neighbors began moving away, most going to the East End, some moving further west to Jackson Ward, or even further out to the West End, while only a small percentage moved to the Northside of Richmond.

Finally, our grandmother, Mama, found a very large house available at 2700 East Grace Street, in the Church Hill area. We all eagerly packed and moved in—my mother and stepfather, who were expecting a newborn, my three siblings and I, one uncle, two aunts and their children, along with one great aunt.

My immediate family lived in the basement of our new home. Mama and Aunt Marge, with her son Theo, lived on the first floor. Marge, the youngest of all of Mama's children, was nine years my senior. Marge loved to dance while gazing at herself in the mirror, performing this narcissistic ritual several times a day, till one morning when her long beautiful hair caught fire from a small heater used to warm the bathroom. It took a long time for her to muster the courage to look in the mirror again.

Aunt Liz and her three girls, Barb, Nora, and Viv, took up residence on the second floor. These three cousins were about the same ages as my two oldest sisters and me. Aunt Liz was a beautiful package of contradictions. Her long hair, slim figure, and smooth, soft chocolate skin, belied her fiery nature, and many a male moth got burned in her flame. She was strong and independent, to the point of being controlling, and though she could be kind, she could also become abusive with the men in her life.

Uncle Billy Buck also came to live with us, and he too resided on the second floor. I remained leery of him, still smarting from our encounter at the party, but as time is a quick healer of youthful wounds, I found myself falling into the web of charm he continued to spin, watching him gain a new coterie of female fans, still awed with the stories he would tell of his experiences during the war. And he was an asset, despite being temperamental, because he would clean the whole house, including the basement sometimes, and would cook for himself or anyone in the family who wished to enjoy the simple but tasty concoctions he would prepare.

My great aunt Nora's room was on the third floor, and as she had a physical disability, she spent most of her time there, wheeling about, taking care of as much of her own personal needs as possible, with Mama providing supplemental care. Aunt Nora was very light-skinned, with silver-gray hair that hung midway down her back, when she let it loose from the ball or French roll in which she wore it most of the time. Sometimes neither she nor Mama would cut her nails for a while, and they would grow long and pointed.

Also on the third floor were Aunt Mattie and my three cousins Rico, Sam, and Nette. Aunt Mattie was also very light-skinned, with freckles on her face. But because so many of the family were dark-skinned, Mattie felt different, and always considered herself the "black sheep" of the family. Nevertheless, she was vain in her encounters with men, who greatly admired her heavy chest, and spoiled her due to her many physical charms. She was very assertive, especially in the defense of her children, and she had a temper that flared whenever she believed an injustice was being committed, either towards herself or anyone else.

So here we all were, a large familial assortment of sizes, shapes, hues and personalities, living under one roof for the first time in a new and unfamiliar section of the city. After the dust settled, we got on with our stabilizing routine of daily living. Goo gave Mama a monthly fee, enough to pay our part of the utilities and monthly rent payments. We kept the basement very clean, sweeping the "floor" that was basically soil so much that it became very hard, especially during the summer months.

But there was still time for childhood play, and we would creatively devise different games to play with the simple materials at hand. The boys would cut branches from trees and pretend they were horses, riding them as cowboys and Indians. We would then shoot at each other with imaginary arrows, arguing over how long we should lie on the ground when shot before re-entering the "battle" (some of the wounded were jumping up too fast after being "hit").

Another favorite game was "Mama and Papa." I would always play the role of Papa and I would send the "children" out to play for a short time, allowing me the opportunity to kiss the beautiful little girl who always played Mama. She lived around the corner from our house, and was becoming a suitable replacement for Kookie, though never occupying the same place in my heart that my first "love" had.

It was at this time that I also learned how to cook, beginning a lifelong love of the culinary arts. Goo would prepare dinner, and I would help her by cleaning the pots, then beating the batter for a cake or pie. When she set her cake or pie in the oven to bake, I would use the top from a mayonnaise jar as my little pan, placing residue of batter in the top, and placing it in the oven beside my mother's larger pan. Then when my sisters showed no interest in the kitchen set mother purchased for them, it was passed on to me, and I delightedly used it to help Goo cook.

I also became close to my Aunt Nora at this time, who preferred me of all the children to go to the corner store for her (one block away) to purchase the few items she might need. Although I didn't always feel like going, I relished the tip she would give me, a tip some of my cousins would vie for, always losing out to me as the chosen errand boy. I gained more than just a tip upon my return. Aunt Nora would invite me to sit down in the chair next to her bedroom window, then from her wheelchair, she would regale me with stories about our family, stories of how slavery had affected her parents and grandparents, stories passed to her as a child as she sat shucking beans with her mother, grandmother, or aunt before a blazing fire, in the dead of winter, when all of nature slept, and the past came alive on withered tongues speaking ancient truths to young ears, passing a treasure of memories to her to store in her heart until time to retrieve each shining jewel for the next generation, presenting them newly polished in fresh communal narrative, a priceless gift I accepted reverently.

Aunt Nora also was the one who first enlightened me to the presence of black people in the Bible. She told me that Jesus was a black man, referring to the description of Jesus in Revelations as having "hair of wool" with "eyes like a burning flame", "his feet like burnished bronze when it has been refined in a furnace."

Another reason I liked going to the store for Aunt Nora, or Mama, or Goo, was because I was constantly finding money lost on the sidewalks or strewn in the grass. So I developed the habit of always looking down as I walked, not out of low self-esteem as some supposed, but rather with the anticipation of finding something. So my trips to the store were lucrative in many ways.

Shortly after our move we were enrolled in Bellevue Elementary School, which was four blocks from where we lived on Grace Street. By this time, my shyness had receded, and I excelled in all my subjects, receiving As for my first academic year at Bellevue. Mrs. Cunningham was my favorite teacher that year, and I would always arrive at school a little early in anticipation of seeing her.

My initial enjoyment of walking to school was marred one morning when I fell, ripping a big hole in the left leg of my pants. All day at my desk, I was disturbed by visions of my mother scolding me for ruining my pants. I was petrified as the dismissal bell rang, and all the way home I rehearsed excuses for the big hole splitting the side of my pants. Some of the other children laughed at me, but I was too worried about mother's reaction to care anything about their jeers.

As I ran through the kitchen door, hoping to sneak down the basement steps before she saw me, she suddenly appeared out of the pantry, carrying a coconut cake on a platter to set on the table. We bumped into each other, and the top of the cake sideswiped my face, covering my cheeks and lips with white icing and flecks of coconut. The sight of me dripping with frosting made her howl, and I joined in, forgetting all about my pants as she wrapped her arm around my shoulder. And to my surprise, when she finally noticed my torn pants, she didn't scold me at all, but simply reminded me to be more careful. I was so relieved, I didn't even care anymore that I had ruined my favorite new pants.

Goo soon gave birth, and we all fell in love with my third sister, Demi, born one December afternoon, an intelligent, pretty, agile little burst of new life, wrapped in a pink baby blanket, as outside Mother's hospital room window the perfectly chilled quilt of winter covered the slumbering earth, its icy white patches glistening under the brief fiery intrusion of the afternoon sun, valiantly blazing before descending back into the blue-gray mists of solstice.

It was to be a sobering season for me, but its lessons strengthened me, preparing me for the overwhelming darkness through which I would later pass. One afternoon, when my mother had gone shopping in downtown Richmond, my second sister Jamie found a twenty-dollar bill under the kitchen stove. I persuaded her to accompany me to the five and dime store on 25th Street, five blocks from our house. There, Jamie fell in love with a beautiful doll that she just had to have, while I was intrigued by a set of white pearl-handled guns, growing excited over the prospect of holding them the next time I played cowboy. We told the salesman we wanted to purchase the doll and guns and after I paid him, we left the store and headed home, jumping up and down in our excitement, half-running, half-walking with our new purchases.

We ran inside the house to find Mother had returned from shopping. With her eyes beaming, Jamie showed Mother her doll and told her about my set of guns. When she found out where we had found the money, she kindly but firmly informed us that the money didn't belong to us, so we didn't have the right to spend one penny. She told us we would be punished, but first she instructed us to return the toys to the store and get her money back.

Reluctantly and fearfully, we returned to the store, where to our surprise the salesman would not accept the toys, and we returned home without all of Mother's money. The saying "finders keepers, losers weepers" certainly wasn't true in our case, and I never found anything again that I didn't immediately return or attempt to return to the person or place that lost it.

Then one Sunday evening, I found myself wrapped in divine protection yet another time. I hadn't felt well all day, but no one in the family paid much attention, as I was frequently stricken with bouts of illness from which I would quickly recover. But that evening, I experienced excruciating pains in my side, and Mama told Goo to get me to the hospital immediately. Without delay, Goo had someone drive me to the emergency room at St. Philip's Hospital, the city hospital reserved for "colored" patients.

I recall the doctor pulling rubber gloves on his hands, then smearing them with some sort of lubricant. He stuck his finger into my rectum, and then said to my mother, "If you had arrived here one minute later, he would have died." This was because my appendix had ruptured, so they carried me into surgery immediately.

When I awakened, I was in Dooley's Hospital for Children, with tubes in both nostrils and all sorts of medical apparatus around me. My room was directly across from the burn ward of the hospital, and at times I could smell the odor that continued to linger even as the children's bodies were recovering. It was very difficult for me lying there, the smell of the badly burned children filling my nostrils with stench, filling my heart with pity for their plight.

In addition, I became extremely frustrated with the tubes in my nostrils, as every time I would drink some liquid, even a small quantity, it felt like the tubes were penetrating deeper into my stomach. Looking at all the medical machines and the bags of toxins being eliminated from my body added to my despondency, so one day I decided to pull the tubes out of my nostrils, which turned out to be an all-day venture.

When the nurse came into my room later that evening and discovered what I had done, she immediately called the doctor, who decided to put the tubes back in place without giving me any anesthesia. Six or seven doctors and nurses had to hold me down during this painful and seemingly lengthy procedure, but this "tough love" therapy cured me of ever trying to remove the tubes again. And as I healed from my surgery, I even began going over to the burn ward to see some of the patients, attempting to cheer them up with my presence, silently praying for their recovery as I sat next to their charred little bodies.

I was discharged two months later, to the amazement of the doctors, who hadn't anticipated such a speedy recovery. But I knew I was rising up on a lot of bended knees—Goo, Mama, family and friends—and my heart swelled with gratitude and love. The students and faculty were overjoyed when I finally returned to school, and I was able to catch up with my classmates, completing all my assignments on time.

It was with tremendous anticipation that I watched my mother bringing my first brother, Walt, home from the hospital, his large brown eyes popping out of his tiny face, his head covered in a little blue baby bonnet. Walt was born one and a half year after our sister Demi. Several days later, Mother brought us children together and asked us if we would like to keep our last name, or change it to our stepfather's last name, as they had decided to get married. We decided to retain our original name, as this is how we were known in school. So they married shortly after that day, making our stepfather our legally official father as well, though in reality he had already assumed his role some time ago.

He continued working in the shoe department of a prominent clothing store in downtown Richmond. Arguments began to ensue between my mother and her husband, as she wanted him to repair the family's shoes at no cost, while he was afraid his supervisor would find out, costing him his job. He frustrated my mother with his lack of response to her heated demands, but he did not like to argue. So sometimes he would repair the soles and heels of our shoes, and other times he wouldn't. Mother wanted him to repair our shoes, as we couldn't always afford new ones, but we had to make do with our father's intermittent repair jobs.

Our father and mother had other problems that stemmed from their vast differences in temperament. Goo had to act as the disciplinarian of the family, as our father never wanted to spank us. There were times when my father had not provided enough money for the rent and my mother would get so angry that she actually hit him, causing us to be afraid he would eventually hit her back, though he never did so.

Goo grew tired of all of us living in Mama's basement, paying her money that could have been used to rent our own house. Week after week, she would challenge our father to look for another house in which to live, but as tensions mounted between them, Aunt Nora suddenly died, leading to a temporary truce, in which Goo was distracted by arrangements needing to be made for Nora's funeral, which Goo was determined would take place in the county of her aunt's birth.

After eighteen months of living in our new home at 2700 E. Grace Street, the landlord told Mama that she would have to move to another house. Mama prayed intently all week, and God answered her fervent prayers when she found a house on Grace Street one block from where we lived! We all moved into the smaller house, but it was very crowded, and we were barely as comfortable as we had been in the previous house. And when Goo's intensified goading of our father to find us another house met with no response as usual, she determined to find us another dwelling herself, and spent what little spare time she had checking with contacts as to where a suitable place for us might be.

In the meantime, I received my first exposure to the ups and downs of entrepreneurship when a neighborhood friend, Tom, and I decided to open our own lemonade business. We took a two-by-four board, nailing each part of a separated skate to each end of the board. Then we nailed a milk crate onto the board as our shelf and storage area. We sold our lemonade at the price of ten cents a cup. But our business venture was short lived; some older boys took all our money and destroyed our mobile business cart, leaving Tom and me both in tears, never to regain our business, for fear of these older boys repeating their atrocities.

In contrast to this disastrous enterprise was a most rewarding encounter with the group of nuns whose living quarters were adjacent to the Catholic school directly across the street from where we lived. Most of the students at this school were white, with only a few black students also attending, so we would wait until all the students were gone for the day then head over to play on the empty school grounds. The nuns were very kind and courteous, as most of the neighbors had been warmly receiving us as new residents in a block that mostly consisted of long-standing members of this community. (There was one particular family, the Pattersons, who thought they were a little better than some of the other residents, and their beautiful daughter carried herself as if she were the Queen of England. But they were the exception rather than the rule.)

So when the nuns would see us playing on the grounds, they would give us cookies and something to drink, especially during the summer when school was not open for students. One day, the Mother Superior invited us to the kitchen door to get some cookies and lemonade. When it was my turn to be at the head of the line, I requested her to let me eat inside the kitchen, an entreaty that drew puzzled looks and murmurings of "you're crazy" from my friends, since I was neither white nor a student.

But to our surprise, she permitted me to come inside and sit down, asking me questions I answered nervously, from the excitement of eating in the kitchen with the Mother Superior and another nun. My curiosity rose, and I dared to ask to be shown more of this interesting house where they lived. Each request continued to be answered graciously in the affirmative.

They showed me their small prayer chapel on the first floor, and as we entered I followed their movements precisely. They each dipped their finger into some water in a container placed on the wall, and then made the crucifix sign on their forehead. I did the same, kneeling in prayer right along with them.

After our prayer, I wanted to know what was upstairs, so they led me up the staircase to their sleeping quarters, showing me the way they cleaned and kept the vestures. I was overwhelmed by their kindness, which seemed to flow endlessly from a bottomless wellspring, and I determined to come here again, to experience the peace, the strangely quiet joy that flowed through every room of their wonderfully peculiar house. I was drawn back again and again, reveling in my long and devoted relationship with these gentle nuns, emanating a power that wordlessly stirred my spirit, silently calling me to join them in an ever-present circle of love.

One day the nuns took me to the school building adjacent to where they lived, and showed me the classrooms for the elementary students. Yet another day, they showed me the building for the upper students, and I assisted them with their cleaning. I wandered through the building, taking in all the sights as I cleaned. As I reached a curtain hanging in one of the rooms, it fell to the floor, revealing a large statue of Mary the Mother of Jesus. Startled by the size of the statue, and stunned by Mary's eyes, which seemed to look through my trembling body to my soul, I ran to the auditorium and fell on the floor. One of the nuns found me, and explained to me how special Mary was, being chosen from all the women on Earth to carry our Lord to His birth. Then she took me to the kitchen where she wrapped a large piece of apple cake for me to take home.

When I arrived home that day, Mother didn't have time to listen to my latest story about the nuns. She was in the kitchen talking with her first cousin Jack, who treated her more like a sister (we children called him Uncle Jack), and was helping her in her endeavor to find another house. I heard her tell Jack that she had finally found what she had been searching for, on 22nd Street, between Broad and Marshall.

So Uncle Jack instructed Goo to find the kind of furniture she wanted for our new house. After Goo found some beautiful yet reasonably priced pieces at Haverty and Gerson Furniture Company, Jack helped her with the very large down payment, continuing to assist her in making the subsequent monthly payments as well. And so we finally moved into our new home—312 North 22nd Street, which unbeknownst to me was right next door to Uncle Lee's house. Mother kept it a secret till moving day, when I delightedly ran up the sidewalk, waving at Uncle Lee as he opened his fence gate and sauntered into our yard with a mischievous grin, scooping me up in his powerful arms. I broke loose and ran up the sidewalk, squealing and jumping.

To a boy used to living in a congested and tumbledown area of Grace Street, this sunny spacious house vastly surpassed the picture I had developed in my puerile imagination. Anticipation rose with each delight that fed my reeling senses, from the fragrant green grass sparkling in the afternoon sunlight, spreading through the front and back yards like a brilliant emerald sea, to the long and shady front porch on which Jack had placed my little rocker and Mother's big one.

I eagerly ran into the large living room, and gasped at the stylish new furniture, which I was seeing for the first time. The sun shone through the as-of-yet bare windows, making two round circles of light on the green sofa. Next I made my way past the stairs and into a medium-sized kitchen, replete with modern accessories—new refrigerator and gas stove, plus the oaken table and chairs that Goo had bought. I circled back and sprinted up the stairs to see where my room would be. (Yes, I was to have my own room at last!) It turned out to be in the rear of the house, while my sisters also had a furnished room of their own. Goo and Shorty (my father's nickname) had the first room to the right as you walked up the stairs to the second floor. Each of us was responsible for cleaning our own room, a chore I performed with relish, considering it small payment for my newly found solitude.

It was at this time that a surprising development took place, which taught me that even a good man can be corrupted if the wrong association continues long and hard enough. Shorty, still repairing shoes at a downtown clothing store, began to socialize with Aunt Marge's husband Charles. The tension between him and my mother apparently escalated to the point where he needed to seek release through male companionship and, in this case, its resultant imbibing. He began coming home long enough to quickly and quietly eat his supper (barely speaking to my mother), only to just as quietly ease out the back door, where Charles would be parked in the alley in his brand new sky-blue Chevrolet.

Many a night I would be awakened by his and Goo's voices

in some sort of discussion about these nocturnal binges with Uncle Charles. No one yelled, but Goo's voice was raised enough to where I could catch snippets of her side of the conversation, such as reminding him he'd always been such a good example, "don't mess it up now that we're heading down movin' up street," my father replying with softer, undistinguishable words. Then we'd all drift off to sleep, till the next night or so, when it would happen all over again. Although it was disconcerting to watch my father slip from the pedestal on which I had placed him, in a way it made me feel closer to him, as he became more human in my eyes, subject to the same weaknesses and temptations as the rest of us "mortals."

During the first year in the new neighborhood, Mother had another boy child, and named him Coy. From a child's perspective, life had definitely improved. School was only two blocks from where we lived, our home was securely wedged between our cousins to our right and the very friendly Wickens family to our left. And since some of our classmates lived around the corner, we were able to forge new friendships quickly. At this time I was nine years old.

There was one great blight on my happiness — in the form of four boys, who stepped out of the shadows of an alley one day to severely test the resolve of one loudly beating but determined heart against eight pounding fists and eight kicking feet. I habitually passed through this alley as a shortcut to school. There were some large dumpsters on the right, surrounded by boxes full of assorted junk. I had passed through this alley day after day without incidence, though obviously my routine had been surreptitiously observed by my predators, hidden and planning to soon pounce on their prey.

So early one crisp fall morning, when the pale sunlight barely penetrated the dim alleyway, four boys rose one at a time from behind the dumpsters. I froze, looking up into the bulbous eyes of a tall boy with a long droopy face, his hands in the pockets of his raggedy brown coat. With him were two short, stocky boys and one other tall slim boy, all of them staring blankly at me, as I stood there stock-still and unblinking. Finally, the tallest boy with the droopy face sauntered over, followed by his three cronies. They formed a circle around me, their bodies brushing mine, the tallest boy's eyes on my lunch bag, the others continuing to silently watch my face.

My heart was pounding, and I began breathing heavily. One of the other boys had foul breath, and since he was my size, he was blowing it directly towards my nose, making me nauseous. I felt a sick coiling in my stomach, and was afraid I might throw up on one of my antagonists, further fueling their hostility, causing them to beat me to a pulp, which I was afraid they were planning to do anyway. For an agonizingly long fifteen seconds or so, we stood there like statues. The tallest boy, who had been popping gum and blowing bubbles over my head, stopped—his eyes going down to my bag, then up to my eyes again. He stuck out his hand, wordlessly commanding me to relinquish the food Mama had fixed me. Reluctantly, I handed it over, angry with them, but more angry with myself for giving in.

He stuck out his hand a second time. "Money," was all he said. I fished in my pocket, and handed him the quarters I was going to use to buy candy and soda after school. I passed through the parting circle of boys, their raucous laughter following me up the sidewalk, and turned left, furiously stomping the pavement all the way to the schoolyard. Yet I never mentioned this incident to my parents or my sisters, as they had all admonished me at different times to stand up for myself, even if it meant getting into a physical altercation. So my shame silently grew as I continued to be robbed by the four nameless boys, cajoling several classmates into giving me half a sandwich or sharing an apple rather than have to admit to my family that mine were being taken.

Finally my pride and my empty stomach had had enough. I woke up very early one morning, after a night of tossing and turning through nightmares in which Mama made all my favorite foods, then handed them to the four boys, who had come to the kitchen door, the tallest one pulling a gun and demanding change she kept in a cookie jar (the same jar from which she gave me quarters every school day.) I woke up exhausted, but my fear had turned to resolve. As I approached the alley that morning, I knew I was going to fight all four thieves, even if it killed me.

I became very nervous as I approached the dumpsters (some days they would be there, some deliberately not, to keep me psychologically off balance). I stopped a moment, not hearing a sound, took a deep breath, then began stepping, my hands balled up into fists at my sides. The first head poked up, then the others. They all wore dark blue skullcaps, as if signifying their group as some sort of junior gang. Their hands were in their pockets; their exhaled breath could be seen in the freezing air.

I waited till they began their customary walk over to me, and as they began to encircle me, I reached down diffidently for my lunch, as if about to hand it over as always, then I kicked the tallest boy in the groin area, grabbing the two stocky ones and showering blows on them with my fists, while kicking the fourth boy, who was creeping up on me, hard in the shins with my shoe. Surprised at my own fury, I continued hammering faces and bodies with my fists, felling one boy into the gravel with a ferocious blow. As the others all ran, he got up shakily and hobbled down the alley after his retreating band.

I chased after them and caught two of them, beating each one down into the gravel, reveling in my sudden victory. Then something came over me as I raised my foot to kick them, as they lay there bloody and stunned. I looked at their scared faces and saw my own, looked at my raised foot and saw that I had become like them. So I lowered my foot and helped them up to their feet. It turned out their names were Rob and Buster, the other two were Willie and Rusty. Ironically, we went on to become the best of friends, and have remained so throughout our lives.

And along with the occasional fights, my sisters and I had a lot of fun with our neighborhood friends and classmates as well. In the evenings, we would play all the childhood games of the day—spin the bottle, postman, picking cherries, hide-and-seek, jack rocks, hopscotch, tag, kickball, baseball—we were a lively group, and played as hard as we studied. If we failed to clean our rooms or the designated parts of the house we were assigned to clean, or if we failed to do our homework, we weren't allowed to go out and play, a powerful motivator in keeping us clean and orderly A students.

The older boys and girls among our group acted as our first mentors, teaching us boys how to fight, and teaching all of us the latest songs and dances. They also taught us how to dress and fix our hair in the latest styles. Some of the older boys wore bellbottom pants with white tee shirts, like sailors, and they straightened their hair into "conks" (the conk style, whose name derived from the hair product name Conkoleen, was made from a type of copal or resin, normally used in varnishes and lacquers.) There was a radio jingle out at the time that proclaimed, "If your hair is short and nappy, Conkoleen will make it happy." One boy, who left the chemical brew on his hair too long, was "happily" left with a bald head for a month! (A common misconception continues that we were trying to emulate white men by straightening our hair. Actually, this style was reminiscent of the Hispanic male stars of the forties and fifties, such as Desi Arnaz, Ricardo Montalban, and Anthony Quinn. It had nothing to do with wanting to be white. We, along with anyone else, just wanted the freedom to be ourselves, to express who we were.) The girls wore dresses and pressed their hair, many of them coming over to the house to have their hair fixed by Goo. Nights found us over on the steps of a supply warehouse building, which was directly across the street from our house. Owned by the Richmond Public Schools, the grounds were very safe, with light poles strategically located for our various games, such as stickball.

During the summer, we would go to The Farmer's Market, located on Franklin Street between 17th and 19th streets. We'd wait until the trailer drivers fell asleep (many often did), then send the smallest child to go through the smallest box on the trailer, stealthily handing out watermelons, cantaloupes, and tomatoes to the rest of us on the sidewalk, while the owner slept peacefully. Leaving watermelon rinds on the sidewalk, we'd return satiated to 22nd Street. Sometimes our parents would shop at The Market later the same day and see the evidence of our crime still lying there collecting flies, so when they noticed our much diminished appetite at supper, they'd query us to see if we'd been involved. But we always denied any part in the stealing, naming some of our older friends as the likely culprits.

My education in thievery continued under the tutelage of my cousin Rita, who enlisted Roy, our cousin, and me in her nefarious assignment at a supermarket located a few blocks from our house. Rita went along with us, and pressured me to go along with their plan, so as frequently occurred, I found myself torn between my desire to please my peers and my desire to please Goo, who I knew would be disgraced by my delinquency (not to mention my growing apprehension of the whipping I was bound to receive). After placing peer acceptance above my own conscience, I helped Roy grab the "assigned" goods, hiding them under our coats, and walking out unobtrusively. But afterwards, I told Roy and Rita very firmly that I would never do that again. They apparently knew I meant business, as they never asked me along again.

Roy was one of my most frequent companions that summer. We roamed the sidewalks during the day, jumping the cracks so as not to "break our mothers' backs"; and pulling cute little girls' braids in a negative attempt to gain attention. After visiting some of our neighborhood friends, we would come back and get the garden hose, each of us holding it in turn, while the other quenched his hot flesh in a stream of deliciously cold water. Then we would sit on the front porch and dry off.

One afternoon, Roy and I sat rocking. He always took my mother's rocker and I was in mine. We rocked squeakily back and forth, watching the neighbors out in their yards, as withered in the fiercely pouring sun as the drooping flowers they listlessly tended. Goo had given us some Cokes from the icebox and a bowl of ice with our glasses. I plopped some cubes into my glass, then poured the Coke over them, listening to it fizz, greedily gulping it down my parched throat. Beads of sweat popped out of my face, pouring down my neck and shoulders, then down my back along my spine—cool relief in the choking humidity.

I looked over at Roy, who was lying back in Mother's rocker with his eyes closed, lazily taking sips from his bottle. He pulled out a wet white handkerchief from his pocket and wiped his face. His black skin was smooth and rich, his cracked lips poked out proudly on his small face. When he smiled, he pulled his lips back so high and wide you could see all his back gums and empty tooth sockets. He ate so much sugar it was amazing he had a tooth left. Sweat poured down his body, plastering his torn brown tee shirt and blue cotton pants against his skin. He reached for the end of his shirt and pulled it off, slinging it over his right shoulder.

I picked up my Coke bottle from the tray and laid it against my hot cheek. Roy, who had opened his eyes, did the same. (I was the unofficial leader of our duo.)

"Muggy out here."

I sighed. "Yeah, I hate a day that sticks to your ribs."

He found this amusing, and he grinned, his near toothless smile resembling a jack-o-lantern's. Sweat continued pouring down his body in torrents and he shook it off his hands as he raised his bottle for another swig. I closed my eyes again, drowsy, orange dots of sunlight dancing under my lids as I drifted to sleep—

A blue jay's cacophony stirred Roy and me from our dozing. He slipped his shirt back on, and started down the porch steps, calling over his shoulder, "Come on, let's go get into somethin'. What are we? Two old ladies sleepin' till supper time?"

With that, we bounded down the sidewalk, ready for whatever adventure presented itself to our eager spirits. Roy ran ahead of me, his pencil-thin legs flying as he jumped into puddles of water left from last night's thunderstorm. He bowed low as he ran ahead of me, his water-filled shoes squeaking like splattered mice.

People were bustling in the mid-afternoon sunshine, getting into their trucks and cars to go downtown or to market. Dogs scampered around the yards we passed, running and sniffing each other. A green Ford shot past, splattering my pants with puddle water, some children in the back seat plastering their faces against the window like fish in an aquarium. One rolled the window down and stuck his tongue out at us, causing me to yell, "Fish Face!" and do the same.

We headed down a path that led through an empty lot on the corner of the next street, the grass and weeds growing thick and high on either side of us as we made our way to the ancient moss-covered tree that stood majestically in the corner. Then we settled in under "our tree," leaning against its thick strong trunk, relishing the cool shade spreading beneath its myriad twisting limbs, songbirds flying in and out of its branches, their warbles the only sound.

Every boy should have such a tree as ours, a secluded shelter where he can get away from grownup eyes, and plan and dream, confiding recent crushes to his best pal, while birds fly above, whistling and chattering. So we lay against the trunk, cooling off our hot bodies and dreaming dreams, some to be shared, some to be kept even from our mothers.

"I'm bored," Roy related, pulling up long blades of grass and throwing them towards an approaching squirrel, which scampered away. I didn't answer him, as I was lost in a reverie, contemplating, as usual, how I could best make the quarters in my old mayonnaise jar grow this summer.

"Did you hear what I said?"

"Yeah, I heard you. Say, a boy in my class says his older brother bought some goldfish, then he got some clear bowls and filled them with water; he set them up on a table in his backyard and he charged—"

"There you go again, chump change dreamin'! If you're gonna dream, dream big! Fish!" He wrinkled his nose. "You want big money, you got to get on at Philip Morris or somethin', and you can't do that till you're older."

Now I turned up my nose. "Cleanin' smelly tobacco? No, thank you, no" I tucked my hands beneath my head, watching a puffy cloud roll by. "I've got to be my own man. I don't want to work for anyone else!"

"You're crazy! You know that? A nine-year-old crazy man! Say, why don't we get some gigs with Old Man Price? My brother worked there one summer—saved enough to get that down payment on his Chevy."

I didn't think I would care to work for Mr. Price, a seemingly grumpy white man who owned the corner grocery store at the intersection of 22nd and Broad streets. "Now who's talking crazy? I'm telling you, these goldfish sold like hot cakes."

Roy would have none of my latest scheme, jumping up and bounding back down the path. "C'mon, slow poke!"

I sighed, reluctant to leave our cool oasis, but obligingly ambling along behind my restless friend. We headed back up the sidewalk, the sun searing my back through my thin cotton tee shirt. A charcoal-grey cat crept out of a yard, stopping in front of us, looking up and blinking his green eyes. I leaned over and tried to pet him, but he hunched his back up and hissed at me, trying to strike my hand with his claws. I pulled my hand away before he could scratch me.

"C'mon, scratch me, see what you get, you mouse eater!" Roy raised his shoe, threatening to kick the cat, which hissed again and jumped towards Roy's leg. We sprinted and barely escaped being bitten and clawed.

"You leave my cat alone! You boys come back here!" Mrs. Ampley had come through her fence gate, and was standing on the sidewalk calling after us. A large, formidable widow, she took no "stuff" off the neighborhood children. And it was true, some of the boys did molest the cat, which contributed to his meanness, but we never had. I turned and called

119

over my shoulder, "We didn't bother your old cat—he tried to bite us!" I glanced at her glaring at me, her gray hair falling in wisps from her bun, holding her precious cat close to her heavy bosom, heaving up and down under her sleeveless yellow apron. She was rubbing her cat's head consolingly.

"Get on home you no-good scamps!" she yelled, going back through the gate, screaming further invectives.

We ran till we reached the corner, folks turning around to see what all the commotion was about, children briefly stopping their play to point and laugh. We stood on the corner, out of breath, and laughing at ourselves, slapping each other on the shoulder in "macho" gusto, rejuvenated by the adventure we'd been looking for all day.

"I'm hungry. Come on over and have supper. Then we can catch some fireflies," I told Roy. "Race you to your door! Ready- set—"

We whirled around the corner, flying down to Roy's house neck and neck, separating as we sprinted past some girls playing hopscotch, coming together and arriving at the Turners' fence at the same time. Roy shook his head, ever amazed at my ability to pump my short legs hard enough to keep up with his runner's lanky frame. But as Goo always said, "You're the most determined child I ever had, Willie."

Mrs. Turner was out in the yard trying to revive some of her drooping azalea bushes. "You having supper with us, Willie?" she asked me, turning off the hose and fiddling with some leaves on the bush, red flowers hanging their parched heads over the baking grass. She sprayed water around several other bushes, one with white azaleas, one with pink, both drooping leaves, some already fallen into the grass along with pink and white petals.

"No, Mama," Roy told her, "we came to ask if I could go over to Willie's to eat."

"Again? You were just by there several days ago. Willie's Mama's gonna get tired of seein' your hard head!" She teased her son, cupping his face with her free hand.

"Stop it, Ma," Roy protested, we being at the age when boys began to resent their mothers being affectionate in public—after all, we now had our image to maintain.

"Go ahead. But Willie, I'll be expecting you to join us next week."

"It's a deal, Mrs. Turner."

"I'll have cat stew, just for you!"

We had turned to leave, but her verbal jab stopped us in our tracks, Roy staring down at the grass and wincing.

"I told you about foolin' with those folks' animals—keep on grabbin' cats' tails!"

"Ma." Roy wheeled around. "We didn't—"

She dismissed him roughly with her free hand. "Go on boy, I got work to do."

Anxious to leave, we darted off without further protests of our innocence. News spread faster than grease on a hot skillet through our neighborhood, and any misdeeds, real or imagined, always made it home before you did. And sometimes the story gained extra episodes by the time it reached parental ears.

"Don't be out late!" we heard her calling as we scampered down the sidewalk back to my house.

Mother let us eat our supper at the picnic table in the backyard, while she and my sisters had their cold plates on the front porch. We played stickball for a while, waiting for it to get dark enough for the fireflies to appear, so we could scoop them up from the air with our Mason jars. But since we'd been doing this all summer, I decided it was time to do some exploring—and of course, when boys explore, mischief's never far behind.

We headed down the alley behind our house, ignoring Mother's instructions to stay in the yard. As we approached the cleaners down towards the end of the alley on the other side, I noticed someone had jimmied open the back window. I motioned for Roy to follow me through the window, and we climbed in, only to discover that the place had been ransacked. So we hurried back out, in case someone showed up and thought we had something to do with it.

But we weren't satisfied with leaving well enough alone. The cleaner's roof was too accessible for two daring boys to decline climbing. So up we went, having a frolic running on the roof, picking up some lose rocks and throwing them down below into the gravel. The open window made an inviting target, so we started throwing rocks through the opening, triggering the alarm system. We jumped off the roof, and ran to our respective homes, sirens blaring in the distance.

After this fiasco, I decided I should get a job to stay out of trouble, and suggested to Roy that he do the same. So Roy and I went to Mr. Price and asked for work. Since Roy had lived in the neighborhood two years and was better known to the owner, he hired him but declined to employ me. But Roy only worked there three weeks before deciding he'd had enough of Price, with whom he didn't get along at all, so he quit one Friday.

So I determined to finally attain this job for myself. It was raining that night, and Mr. Price was stuck with approximately 200 bags of coal to be unloaded, and no helper. So as he stood by his station wagon unloading bags in the pouring rain, I asked him if I could help him unload all this coal. So this time, he put me to work and even told me to report the next day, which was Saturday.

This gave me a chance to show him what a fireball I was when it came to work, not to mention my facility in speedily adding dollars and cents amounts in my head. The store was packed with customers on Saturday night, and I coolly and quickly juggled various duties, bagging orders, taking children's requests for candy, adding order amounts mentally, and collecting monies for Mr. Price. I took the initiative while performing these tasks, not waiting for Mr. Price's every instruction. He was impressed with my drive and my computational proficiency, informing me at closing time that I had the job permanently.

I was to report to work at 7:30 a.m. weekdays, staying until 8:30 a.m., which would give me time to run to school each morning, a block from the store. Then I would report back after school, working from 4:30 to 9:30 p.m. Saturdays I worked 7:00 a.m. to 9:30 p.m., Sundays 8:30 a.m. to 1:00 p.m., returning from 4:30 to 9:30 p.m. I was nine years old when I started working for Mr. Price at $20.00 a week. For the next two years, I worked every day except two half-days at Thanksgiving, two Christmas days, and one day off not connected to a holiday. Needless to say, my plan to stay out of trouble succeeded, and the quarters in my Mason jar changed to bills.

Another year passed when my mother gave birth to another boy, naming him Monte. I was happy to have this cute little brother, though sometimes he kept me up at night with his crying.

Then on January 3, 1957, Felicia was born and brought home on a very cold and dreary day. But she was pure sunshine, and Aunt Liz took one look at her and dubbed her "Peanut," because she was a tiny cocoa-butter brown bundle, with very smooth skin. Felicia was the joy of the family, even though she was the fourth and last of the girls to be born. Everyone got caught in the web of winsome ways she innocently weaved. She cried even more than Monte and

123

loved to be held. She got her wish, because all of us loved to hold her and watch her little face light up as she cooed and gurgled. Her godmother was Emma, Goo's best friend from the old neighborhood. And Demi, a mere two years older, tended Peanut as if she were her mother. Other family members acted as nurturing surrogate parents, as well as doting older sisters, Aunt Liz, who would frequently stop by and play with her, and even Walter, who started coming home earlier than usual, going out with his friends less and less. And I shared as much time as I could with our newly formed jewel, including Demi in our play, as she was still in need of special attention.

With all the happiness Felicia (whose name means happiness) brought our family, we were blissfully unprepared for the tragedy that played itself out all too soon. It all started so harmlessly, so routinely. One Saturday, Goo went downtown to purchase clothes for the family. I believe my sisters were either outside or on the first floor, my father lying intoxicated in one of the second floor bedrooms, while Demi and Monte were playing in a room heated by a coal and wood stove, the door of which was partially open. Monte crawled across the floor, much too near to the hot stove, so Demi ran over and picked him up, a fiery red piece of coal falling onto the end of her dress as she did so. She ran through the house screaming, though amazingly unable to rouse Walter from his stupor. Someone did run upstairs to help her—Uncle Buck, only to see her engulfed in fire. We rushed her to the hospital, where we learned she had third-degree burns over eighty percent of her little body. Anger and grief consumed Goo, who lambasted Walter for being too drunk to respond to Demi's screams, screams that Uncle Buck said "were loud enough to wake the dead." Nor would she allow us children to visit her until a week later.

My first visit was not as bad as I had anticipated. As Goo and I entered the hospital unit for burn victims, I expected to see a miserable and moaning Demi, but instead we were greeted with her beautiful contagious smile and usual optimistic wit. As we listened to the assurance in her voice, despite her precarious condition, we began to be encouraged that things would get better for her, even expecting her to be released from the hospital before too long. We went home planning to fill Demi's long healing journey with our abundant love and support. Other family members were also hopeful about her return home, and they pledged to do whatever was needed for her recovery.

Following this very positive but only visit of mine with Demi, we received bad news. My mother took the call. She and my father were requested to come to the hospital. When they returned home, she stunned us with her announcement that Demi had died. I was just a boy, with a boy's understanding, but I tried desperately to make sense of what had happened. We had looked forward to Demi's healing—it would have been a long, arduous recovery, but recovery had seemed certain. Now she was dead.

I couldn't comprehend how God could have let this happen—Mama had always taught us He was "full of nothing but love" —how could He let this happen to little Demi, so trusting, so loving? My father sat in his favorite chair, covering his tear-drenched face with his shaking hands. We children tried to comfort each other with mutual hugs, but we remained wrapped in tears. In my increasing bewilderment, I decided maybe an outsider might help me to understand this painful mystery, as my family members were too caught up in their own grief to be able to help me. So I walked to the store and told Mr. Price that Demi had died. He was very sympathetic, and did his best to console me, but I left still devastated. Death, it seemed, had swallowed up our loved one, but unlike Jonah she would not be spit out of the creature's mouth, whole and sound, and we would remain ever isolated from her. Death, the more experienced fighter, had won, it seemed.

Finally, I did what Mama always said to do whenever I was sad or in trouble — I got down on my knees, by my bed, where I hadn't been able to sleep for nights — and I prayed. This was my first intentional appeal to God to help me understand what was going on. I fervently poured out all the questions I'd been carrying in my beleaguered soul. How could Demi die when they said she was doing so well? Did something go wrong in the hospital? Were the doctors to blame for not providing the best medical care? Goo had always worried about Monte, who was born with a hole in his heart, but now Demi, the lively one, was gone. Why?

This was my first query about death and its impact upon both adults and children. During my prayer, I told God that I still loved Him, but I just wanted to understand. As I spoke these words aloud in my pitch-black room, a Presence suddenly filled me — the same Presence that surrounded me the night I prayed for Uncle. Inexplicably, I felt totally loved — and I envisioned Demi totally loved and wrapped in glowing light. I arose, and lay my weary head on my pillow, continuing to envision Demi covered with a light that was including me in its radiance. It came to me clearly in that moment — how, I didn't know — that before she died, God made things better between Him and Demi, so she would be full of joy when she entered this beautiful light. That is why her rising spirit had glowed from within her ravaged body, surrounding her with the aura of life and love. So it was alright to die, if dying meant living in this beautiful love-filled light. I fell asleep, resting in the consolation sent to me on the pleas of my prayer.

During these days, the remains of the deceased would be placed in the home of the family. Demi lay in the first room to the right of the first floor hallway. Each night when I got home from work, I would run past this room, without looking to see who had come to pay their last respects. And I surely didn't want to see Demi lying there; I wanted to remember her as she was, especially holding on to the memory of how animated she was when I visited her in the hospital. On the day of her burial, my mother and father cried like two abandoned babies. Walter drank more and more hard whiskey after Demi's death. Guilt was pulling him apart, we knew, though the family never discussed this.

So the family abided for weeks in a blur of pain and confusion. We got up from snatches of sleep, performing chores and duties by rote, clinging to the remaining remnants of our sanity. But there is a time to grieve, and it cannot—nor should it be—rushed or pushed downward, left to grow and resurface later, with disastrous results.

But we were not alone, as the vision I'd received during my prayer reminded me. Then one morning, I was awakened by a preacher Goo had tuned into on the radio. She did this every morning, but the words just went right through me, though I continued to pray every morning and night, a prayer for the strength just to make it through that day, a prayer just to have a little sleep and its blessed forgetfulness.

But this morning was different. The preacher's words roused me from brief sleep, affording me a strange but heartening dream. I walked past an old country church, and at the edge of the yard stood a single wooden cross. It was raining, and I walked over in front of the cross, watching the water pouring down its bark onto the ground. I walked further down the road, and read the street sign—Hollow Road.

I turned off the road, and wandered down a narrow dirt path that led through cold, dark woods to a river bank, lighted by cascading light, yet with no sign of any sun in the crystal sky. On the other side of the water walked a small figure, whose face was covered with a mask, with only the narrowest of slits for the eyes and mouth, which I could barely make out. The figure had on a flowing white gown, and walked by the river, stepping barefoot through the green grass. The figure bent over, struggling unsuccessfully to remove the stifling mask. I felt sorry for this figure and wanted to help, but couldn't move from where I stood on the other side of the river, watching, helpless to keep the figure from suffocating. Finally, I stretched out my arms to indicate to the figure how much I wanted to help but couldn't. The figure straightened up and familiar eyes looked right into mine. The figure pulled off the mask—it was Demi. She stood on the bank staring at me—not smiling, but serene and free. I waved to her, trying to get her to smile; and as she smiled, she extended her arm, pointing her finger to beyond me, to the path I'd just taken—

"…in Our Father's love." The dream merged into the radio preacher's slow cadence. "Nothing can happen without God's direction of His force being behind it."

"Yes," a member called loudly in the background.

"Even from the evil that takes place, God will pull forth a flower of goodness from it."

"Yes," they answered. I lay against my pillow, in rapt attention.

"He will rain His righteousness upon it, and make it grow to an even bigger blossom of goodness."

"Alright, yes," several answered.

"Yes," I murmured, his words evoking Demi standing by the river.

"You who do evil, be aware that God will take the evil you do and turn it around on you to His purpose, and make its end result one of greater goodness that will leave you cringing in fear and shame."

He began to speak faster and louder. "Because God is the Inspirer of all, the Intender of all, the Director of all. Nothing you can do is outside of the Eternal Plan of God—no matter how trivial, no matter how shameful, no matter how self-serving—and no deed you do is hidden from His all-seeing Eye."

Many cries and claps sounded. The preacher's voice became a horn, making eternal clarion call to the lost of all time. "Do not be deceived by the Deadly Deceiver, deceived into thinking that you can do without God. That diaphanous lie has landed many a fly in that old shifty spider's web. So don't be deceived—do you hear me?—into thinking that you are the director. For He knows—the very number of hairs on your head. He knows—the very number of times you have transgressed. He knows—the very number of times you have lusted for your neighbors' wives and daughters."

The congregation was shouting now, responding in waves of spiritual heat to the preacher, a firecracker now, exploding with all the force he could muster, issuing forth his chanted assurance that in spite of our weakness, God was still taking care of His own children.

"...And not only does He know—your every transgression—your every weakness. He knows—the very number of times you have tried and failed. He knows—the very number of times your friends have turned their backs on you and left you 'buked and scorned. He knows—the very number of times you have sat lonely and lost—in the darkness of your solitude, wondering when the light will appear."

I sat up, quickened by the preacher's rousing rhythm; I saw

Goo standing at her dresser in her slip, folding her hands, then raising them to heaven, her eyes closed. "Tell it, tell it," the cries rose up from the members.

He began to whisper loudly. "He knows—when you are in the darkest hour of your long and lonely life—when you sit feeling the pain of every sorrow cut through you like a twisting knife." Suddenly the whisper began to rise into a moan, a moan fraught with anguish for the hovering flock. I sat transfixed. "That is right—He knows—when you can't find a way to bring a light into the dark." He chanted on, riding on the peak of the congregation's rapturous swell. "He knows—when you can't find a way to stop the trembling of your weary heart. He knows—the very number of times you have prayed through your falling tears into the darkness." Cries still rose over thunderous applause. "He knows—the very number of times He's listened to you call His name. And He-ee knows—the number of the day you will die and the day I will die—yes—and He-ee knows—the very number of the day He will reveal Himself to us—and we will know that day—yes, we will know that day—"

"Yes, Lord, yes," they cried.

"And we will know His Plan has been perfected. For He is our Perfecter—" He was winding down now, his fiery rhetoric descending steadily into a steady hiss of steam. "We will know His perfect will that He had set in place all this time, and in Him will you find your own perfection, that which He planned for you—"

He waited for a long burst of applause to subside. He emanated a power that I sensed could not be self-generated, resurrecting my wounded, exhausted spirit, lying lifeless within my young, vibrant body, his feverish voice fanning the flickering flame of my faith into brightly burning fire.

"He will meet you on that day with your very own perfection prepared by His Hand—the perfect you, the perfect I—that He had always lovingly planned for—the perfect us we will be on a perfect day kept hidden for us by Him—" An avalanche of cries and claps tumbled over the preacher's words, a tumult of jubilant voices sounding as one. "On that perfect day, we will see clearly shining before us the Love that now keeps us through every tribulation—and we will see clearly that the Light was shining all the time—shining out from that perfect Love that brought us home safely. "Come home—come home—"

The program abruptly cut off at the top of the hour. We wouldn't hear the inflamed converts surge forward to receive the cooling touch of the preacher's hands, his voice now soft and reassuring, though I was eager for him to walk me further through that "clear shining Light," the Light that had poured onto Demi's shining face, finally cleared from the heavy mask of clay, triumphant and free.

Goo stood before her dresser mirror, slipping her dress slowly over her head, her powerful voice filling the silent house.

"Blessed Assurance, Jesus is mine; O what a foretaste of Glory Divine—"

I picked up my comb from the night stand and briefly ran it through my short-cropped hair, watching Goo pick up the pitcher of water she kept on her dresser top and pour out a glassful, drinking it as she gazed at herself in the mirror. I ran across the hall and hugged her, partially enfolding her wide hips with my arms. She lay her hand on my head. "Everybody's got to make their own journey, Willie. Demi's made hers—made it fine—and she's home now. Now you and I, we've got a little ways to go. We've taken our rest—oh, grief is wearisome, and we have to take our rest—but now we have to get movin' again." She poured me a glass of water. "You understand, Willie? We've got to get to steppin' now!"

I nodded, reaching for the water she handed me. We drank together, refreshed down to our souls.

"Let's go have some tea."

I followed her down the stairs to the kitchen, joining Uncle Buck who was coming out of his room. Uncle took Goo by the arm and escorted her down the hall. Mutual grief had pulled the whole family closer, helping the rift between Uncle and me heal, and we were steadily approaching our previous camaraderie.

The teakettle whistled as we sat at the kitchen table. Goo poured tea into four peach-colored china cups, setting out a plate of warm blueberry muffins. She had also baked a pineapple upside-down cake, which she had set in the pantry to cool, and we sat inhaling the delightful mixture of fruity smells permeating the air. Goo said the blessing, and while she and Uncle closed their eyes, I watched him at prayer, something I seldom saw, though his face remained inscrutable under my gaze. They opened their eyes, and we had our tea, Goo enjoying this welcome respite from dinner preparation.

I always enjoyed helping Goo cook our meals, standing beside her and doing whatever she asked of me, cleaning the pots and pans right after she used them, so we never had to weary about cleaning a sink full of dishes after dinner. I still used the toy kitchen set I had acquired from Zee and Jamie, cooking leftover food Goo gave me. She taught me how to cut up a chicken into quarter or eighth parts and then fry them. I was especially fond of her succulent baked fish, particularly lake trout. We always had fish every Friday— Spanish mackerel, blue fish, salmon cakes or baked salmon with rice. She fixed the fish, and I'd clean the accompanying greens, cooking them to taste.

One day, Goo went downtown and left a large chicken to thaw out in the sink. So I decided to help out by cutting the chicken into parts as she had taught me. The bird was extremely tough, and I finished this laborious task with a sigh of relief. I'd never had such trouble cutting up a chicken before, and attributed my difficulty to the knife being dull, taking it outside and sharpening it on the concrete curb in front of the house. But when Goo returned home, she looked in the refrigerator and asked what happened to the "hen." I told her all the trouble I'd had cutting it up. She laughed, explaining to me the difference between a chicken and a hen, embarrassing me at dinner that night by sharing this episode with the entire family. Goo explained to me that a hen is much tougher than a chicken and you usually bake a hen and fry chicken.

I'd grown to be a strange mixture of domesticity and restlessness, and I began frequently running away from home whenever my wanderlust took me over. It all started one hot summer Saturday afternoon, a routine day with Goo downtown shopping while we children were left at home to clean and do chores. I had the added responsibility of supervising my older sisters and making sure they did everything expected of them, as normally they were the bigger procrastinators. But this Saturday, I fell under their influence, and thinking we could have our fun and still have the house clean when Goo returned three hours later, we played games and even had an impromptu Kool-Aid and cookie party in the kitchen, turning up the radio and dancing to the latest rhythm and blues hits. As I got up to demonstrate some of my moves, I watched my sisters' eyes widen, their mouths opening with surprise. I was a good dancer, but not good enough to merit such looks of astonishment, so I turned around to see Goo standing in the kitchen door with two heavy bags of purchases.

Zee ran and turned off the radio, as we braced ourselves for our beatings. We were ordered to our rooms to wait for our successively rendered floggings. I waited nervously, listening to Zee's usual hysterics. She screamed and hollered as if someone were killing her—even before receiving the first lick—so Goo only hit her two or three times. Then she moved on to the ever-stubborn Jamie, who always ended up receiving more blows. I could hear the belt landing on Jamie's backside, but there was no verbal response from my recalcitrant sibling. Goo apparently was picking up momentum as she hit Jamie, so I figured by the time she got to me, I would really catch a licking. I sat there waiting, staring out the window, startled to suddenly hear Jamie actually crying from the beating. That did it—I decided I would jump out the second floor window, and as Goo approached me with belt in hand, I jumped, the bushes below breaking my fall, though I had cuts and scrapes all over me. She called out the window for me to "get back in the house or else you won't be able to sit down till you're thirty," but I was already halfway down the alley and never looked back.

I ran to a neighborhood hangout for the young folk, a restaurant at 24th and Broad, spending the rest of the day there, talking to various acquaintances and listening to the jukebox, even being treated to hamburgers by several teenagers I knew. Then several of my cousins stopped by, alerting me that Goo was out looking for me and was now only several blocks away. I darted out of there, scampering to the corner of a nearby parking lot, where I slept for two or three hours, not reporting to work as expected. I woke up from a fitful sleep, disoriented, wondering what I was doing in this dark parking lot, rain falling steadily on my aching body. Then it all came back to me—Jamie's cry, Goo with the belt, my jumping out the window.

Cold, wet, and tired, I determined to return home and accept the beating I'd run from. But when at last I walked through the door, Goo and everyone were so happy to see me, all I got were hugs and kisses. Goo gave me something to eat, then I took a long soaking bath. She tended my cuts and bruises, scolding me for "my fool stunt" that could have resulted in serious injury or worse. Then she tucked me into bed, something she hadn't done in a long while.

The next day, we had a heart-to-heart talk about my taking off. She wanted to know if I thought she didn't love me, because of all her discipline, but I told her I knew she loved me dearly, I just didn't want to take my licking at the time. I didn't go to the grocery store that day either, too embarrassed to face Mr. Price, so I was alone enjoying Sunday quiet (the rest of the family had gone to church) when Uncle Jack knocked at the door. We had a long talk, requested by Goo, but the conversation ended with a whipping, much worse than I would have received from Goo, rendering all my efforts at escape in vain.

When I finally returned to work on Monday, Mr. Price said nothing about the incident, but shot me a most disapproving look, which he continued to do throughout the day. Then later that week, he lightened my growing chagrin by teasing me with jokes about my inane escapade. (Little did he know, there were more to come.)

The neighborhood began to change at this time, with a lot of white families moving to the West End of Richmond, or out to the suburbs of Henrico and Chesterfield. A few skirmishes occurred between the older black and white youths, resulting in Mexican standoffs, after which everyone settled down into mutual avoidance. Still, there were a few remaining white neighbors who were very friendly, including Mr. Earl, Mr. Price's father-in-law, who lived above the store. He would come down and talk and joke, though he never interfered in the business aspects of the store. Then there was Fred, tall and athletic, and his heavyset wife, Nancy, who lived a block from the store and were frequent customers. But my favorite white customer was Patsy Echo, who was very jovial with all the customers and employees, including me, and her banter livened up many a dull afternoon.

New loves beckoned to me at about this time, and I went from being forlorn over the lost Kookie to being pleasantly surprised at becoming the bone of contention between two equally determined bite-worse-than-bark female rivals. It all started when I joined in playing community games at a nearby playground. There I encountered the beautiful tan-skinned Sara with big brown eyes who exuded an air of confidence well beyond her years. She was very aggressive, kicking or batting a ball as well as any boy—if not better—and when she wanted something, she went directly and openly after it. She took an immediate and obvious interest in me, which boosted my confidence enormously, as I was still very shy around girls I didn't know well.

I was contemplating asking her to be my girlfriend when I met Nette, who also participated in our games. When I first saw her, she was standing on the sidelines of a kickball game, wearing a beautiful green sweater over an A-line black skirt that accentuated her trim figure. She saw me looking at her, so she smiled, revealing dimples that augmented the natural beauty of her face. I went over to speak to her, and her gentle voice made my heart beat strongly and rapidly. She wasn't as aggressive as Sara, but within her appealing softness and alluring self-containment, I sensed a quiet strength that drew me closer. So I was in quite a romantic dilemma, torn between the bold, adventurous Sara and the serene, assured Nette. I was beginning to lean towards Nette with her gentleness and genuineness. Sara could be overwhelming at times, and I sensed that once I was no longer a challenge, her interest in me would fade. Still, she was a lot of fun, and she continued to bewitch me with her engaging vivacity.

I started purchasing perfumes and other little gifts from the store for both girls, though I still hadn't officially asked either to be my girlfriend. One afternoon, I was walking from school to the store as usual, when I heard a loud commotion coming from further down the street. Folks were gathering to watch some sort of fracas, so I ran to see what was going on. Elbowing my way through the growing group of jeering boys, I made my way to the edge of the sidewalk, stunned to see Sara straddled on top of Nette's abdomen, scratching her face with her long hard nails. Both girls were disheveled and dirty, their dresses torn, their eyes blazing with mutual hatred.

I stood there by the curb, watching this debacle with amazement. Some of the boys behind me started patting me on the back, congratulating me for being "cool" enough to have "two chicks mixing their feathers" over me. I didn't know whether to be proud or ashamed. Up until then, my confidence with girls was too low to even consider that any would actually fight over me. The two girls picked themselves up amid all the masculine hoots and hollers, totally unaware of my presence throughout their intense battle. Suddenly spying me on the sidelines, my mouth wide open in amazement, they both eyed me ruefully, scattering quickly in different directions before I could catch up to either one. This was a lesson to me not to toy with two girls at the same time, although my dalliance was not intentional. I really cared for both girls. Although Nette was the loser of the fight, she was the ultimate winner with me, and she became my official girlfriend—for six months. And she still bears the scar on her otherwise still lovely face.

But romance was not the only trouble spot I was negotiating. Trouble was brewing at home and at school as well. Some of my fellow students began calling me "stinky" due to the fact that they could smell lingering fumes on me from pumping kerosene at the store before coming to school. And if I sat close to the window on a very hot day, they would actually see steam coming from my pant legs in the bright sunlight. This would set off an explosion of laughter that got me into hot water with Ms. Johnson, the decidedly unamused teacher.

But I earned back their respect the day a hysterical student named Elmer threatened everyone in the classroom, including Ms. Johnson, then went and sat on the second floor window ledge, ready to jump. Everyone was frantic, so I approached Ms. Johnson and asked permission to speak to Elmer. As she was at a loss as to how to handle him, she agreed to let me try. I poked my head out and talked to Elmer on the ledge, remembering my own stunt of jumping out of the window into the bushes. Using reverse psychology, I told him calmly and coolly, "Elmer, I know you're not crazy—you must have a very good reason for wanting to jump." His eyes widened in disbelief. "So if you want to jump, I'll help you. I'll give you a little push, and everything will be over. Ready?" Elmer, stunned at my seeming willingness to push him, became frightened as I came even closer. He crawled quickly back through the window and planted his big feet firmly on the classroom floor. Everyone was greatly relieved, but sat at his or her desks in stunned silence, not knowing what to make of Elmer or me. But no one called me stinky anymore, and Elmer and I became very good friends, and still are. Whenever I see him, I go back to that day when I cheerfully told him I'd give him a push, possibly saving his life in the process, and I'm sure I conjure the same memory for him.

Meanwhile, Goo had to stop working, due to a heart condition that was worsening, probably due to the stress of her recent grief over Demi. She was bored sitting around the house all day, as she was a task-oriented lady (a trait I inherited), and always needed to be doing something productive. She began having family, friends, and neighbors over frequently to the house for dinners, giving her a reason to cook food all day, which she thoroughly enjoyed. Most of her guests would bring liquor purchased from the ABC store, eating and drinking for hours.

Though Goo didn't drink, she began to realize the profit that could be made by selling the whiskey herself, instead of folks bringing their own bottles. So Goo joined Uncle Buck and other relatives in selling liquor, despite her previous scorn of such. Uncle Jack was not pleased with this idea at all, and admonished her about the risks involved in pursuing this illegal activity, but her mind was made up—nor could Walter dissuade her, since he was himself drinking heavily at this time. And it did bring in much-needed revenue to our depleted family funds.

As if things were not frenetic enough, I even got myself involved in gang warfare. Late one summer evening, I saw four older boys chasing my cousin Bumpy and his friend Harold down the alley behind the restaurant at 24th and Broad. I picked up a two-by-four board and ran behind the other boys intending to pass it to Bumpy and Harold to use against the boys, as I was much younger and smaller in stature. The older boys heard me following, and turned around together, backing me up against a wrecked car parked in a service station lot on 24th and Marshall streets. One of them pulled a long switchblade out of his back pocket, closing in on me as I leaned against the car, helpless and very frightened, yet managing to maintain my composure. He was very close now—I could smell his liquor-tinged breath. His fierce eyes looked into mine, signaling to me my own imminent death. My heart was racing. I closed my eyes, and began to pray, sweat beads popping out on my face.

Then I heard the voice of one of the other boys—"Wait! He's not the one!" Miraculously, at the same time, Bobby, a family friend who lived across the street, ran out of his house with a pump shotgun, aiming it at my assailants, who ran off in the other direction. In the meantime, someone had run to our house and told Goo and my sisters what they had seen happening to me. So they arrived now as I leaned on the car, trembling with fear, taking my hands and leading me back home.

After hugging me in relief for a full fifteen minutes, Goo gave me a stern lecture about following older boys and getting involved in their fights. Later that night, Bumpy and Harold came by to see how I was doing and to thank me for trying to help them out. (It turned out that the other boys were from Fulton, and neighborhood gang rivalry over who-knows-what was at the root of this night's violent eruption, in which I could have been yet another all too young victim of its senseless bloodshed.) Bumpy and Harold praised my bravery to all their friends, but I didn't feel brave, I just was doing what I felt I had to do to help my kin, regardless of the consequences. And once again, the Lord had responded to my desperate plea for protection.

I was growing up fast, and was now thirteen years old, and another assault happened at the store shortly after this, which opened my eyes to yet another disturbing aspect of life. One

Saturday morning, a frequent customer named Jim ran into the grocery store in a panic. Jim was a very well groomed gentleman, with spit-shined shoes, well-pressed slacks, and starched shirts. He would come into the store every evening, carrying a black umbrella, whether it was raining or not, and a newspaper neatly folded under his arm. He was very articulate, gentle, and kind.

Jim lived at 22nd and Grace, and this particular morning, a man named Red chased Jim into the store, beating him badly. Jim fell into the corner between the counter and the meat case, curled up like a little child, not attempting to fight back or defend himself, lowering his head as Red continued to land blows all over his body. I stood behind the counter, in shock at what I saw between Red and Jim. Mr. Price later shared this strange encounter with some of the other customers, and they revealed to us that Jim was homosexual. I was disappointed to learn this news about this scholarly gentleman whom we'd always admired and it upset me deeply to see such a dignified person so brutally beaten and humiliated. But I never treated him any differently after this, even though I disagreed with his lifestyle. I went out of my way to be nice and respectful to Jim, as he had always been to me, as I'm sure he was most ashamed of what we had witnessed. (Several weeks later, I saw two lesbians, who lived directly behind the store, kissing in front of their living room window. It disturbed me to see this, and I was glad I never encountered Jim being so affectionate with his friend.)

Sad news continued to be dispatched to our family, and I began to think we would never discard the blanket of despair by which we were covered. One Friday evening, I was walking down Broad Street in the rain, eager to have a few minutes to go home and play before reporting to work. When I turned the corner onto 22nd Street, I saw something that pierced my heart. There was all of our furniture, piled on the sidewalk in the pouring rain. I stood there getting soaked, wondering how and why this could have happened. We never received any explanation as to why we were evicted from the home we loved so dearly. We were told we would live with Mama (Grandmother) again, at the corner of 22nd and Grace streets. So Uncle Jack and Uncle Lee helped Goo move with all we could salvage from the rain, and they stored most of our belongings in Mama's garage.

So Goo, Tiny, three sisters, three brothers, and I lived in one room with Mama at 22nd and Grace. This was a drastic change from our house, where I had a room to myself, the baby slept with my parents, and my sisters and brothers respectively shared the other two bedrooms. Now four of us slept in one bed, two sisters at the head, two brothers at the foot, while Peanut and the baby boy both slept with Goo and my stepfather in their bed. The room was large enough to have the two beds, an oil stove, dresser drawer, and closet. All the other furniture remained in the garage, along with some clothing, toys, and other belongings. So we were constantly trooping out to the garage for extra clothing and necessities as the seasons progressed.

But despite the crowding and the many inconveniences it caused, we were fortunate to be located one block from both the school and the grocery store. Being able to keep my same job and attend the same school afforded me the security of familiar surroundings and steady relationships during these otherwise difficult days.

And Mama was extremely kind to us, doing everything she could to make the house she generously shared with her large family into a loving home and a much-needed shelter from the emotional storms through which we were passing. Unfortunately, there were other dwellers in the house who seemed determined to wreck any familial happiness we managed to secure for ourselves.

There was Aunt Marge, youngest of Mama's children and the apple of her eye, constantly bickering with her husband Charles, while Mama ran interference for Marge, when she should have stayed off the playing field. Worse, Uncle Buck had ensconced his new girlfriend Gladys in his room, which was between the living room and kitchen. We dreaded ending up in the midst of personal encounters we wanted no part of. Whether fighting or lovemaking, our appearance would of course anger Uncle Buck and embarrass us, leaving me to wish he had remained the even-keeled Karla's beau, roosting in her luxurious love nest instead of with Mama.

But Karla was too quiet for Uncle, with his strong taste for the tempestuous, and so we were saddled with the fiery Gladys, igniting Uncle's short fuse with relish, her provocations rewarded with busted lips or blacked-out eyes. Goo's house rule was that no one was to interfere in husband-wife altercations, or in fights between other family members, so as not to have us teaming up on each other — unless it reached a point that one of the participants would sustain serious or fatal injury. In other words, we were not to side with a family member who was wrong, but we also were not to neglect to support each other when help was needed. And Mama, who lived on the second floor with Marge and Charles, would never interfere with anything not involving Marge, which is why Uncle always gave Aunt Marge a wider berth than he did the rest of us, knowing the ensuing blood bath that would surely have occurred between him and Mama if he so much as touched her.

Amusing in retrospect, though not at the time, was the nightly urination in the children's bed, perpetrator unknown. Despite our repeated appeals to Goo to demand the identity of the leaky sibling, no one would confess, and with all the other problems she was shouldering at this time, she wasn't about to give priority to our requested bed-wetting investigation. So night after night, I had to lie in my own narrow space, not turning or stretching out for fear of lying in a puddle of urine. Arguments ensued among the siblings, accusations circulated, and I woke up frustrated and cranky from lack of sleep, especially on those mornings when it was my turn to get up early and put more oil in the stove. Finally, the problem resolved itself that spring when the bed-wetting suddenly stopped. I suspect it resulted from the stress of all the accumulated changes we were experiencing, alleviated once the family settled down into a regular daily routine.

This stress worked on the older siblings in a different way. Jamie and I began snapping at each other, arguing over the pettiest of issues. One afternoon, the growing tension between us escalated into a full-blown physical fight. We started off exchanging salty jibes, followed by me chasing Jamie through the house into our room, where she slammed the door in my face, attempting to block my entry by propping a chair under the knob. I broke through, knocking her and the chair into the floor. As I approached, she threw a small can of tomato sauce at my face, cutting my top lip, the blood flowing down my lower face and neck. Furious, I charged at her. "I'm going to kill you," I ranted, as she darted down the hall ahead of me, hiding behind Mama whom we had roused from her daily nap with our entire ruckus.

I stood there, breathing heavily, my lip pounding, blood running down my shirt, Mama glaring at me, Jamie peeping at me from around her right hip. Goo came running in from the kitchen, her hands covered with flour. Jamie immediately squealed that I had chased and threatened her, so she threw the can at me in self-defense. Goo took me to the MCV hospital emergency room, where they stitched the huge gash in my lip. It took weeks to mend, and I had to endure the snickers of several girls I had secret crushes on in the meantime. I also made the mistake of telling a friend of mine what happened, and he spread the news among the boys that a girl had licked me, so I was subjected to their taunts as well. Goo made us promise not to fight again, and with all the embarrassment it had caused me, I readily complied—for a while.

But we ended up in a tussle several months later when Jamie decided to follow in my footsteps and run away from home rather than accept discipline over some infraction. She dashed out the door, running along the park hillside adjacent to our house, then down the slope along Richmond Hill. "Lord have mercy, go get your sister right now—hurry, or you'll both have fiery behinds!" Goo warned. Infuriated that Jamie's stubbornness was mixing us both in a jam, I ran after her with all the gusto within me, catching her by the arm, and pulling her as she tenaciously resisted. "I'm not getting a beating because of you, you mule head!" I yelled. We pulled each other back and forth, landing on the ground in a furious scuffle, which I eventually won, pulling Jamie up with one arm, which I then twisted behind her back, marching her home as she called me every foul name she could think of.

As we neared the house, her pride got the better of her, and she relaxed, persuading me with her demeanor to let go of her arm. She couldn't bear to be seen being coerced by her brother, so I let her walk beside me, as if she were returning of her own volition. Goo, who was posted at the kitchen window, hadn't seen our tug of war on the other side of the hill, or we would have both been whipped for fighting again. But this skirmish served as a release of the built-up animosity between us, and we settled back to being fast friends again.

Spring brought fresh problems and disappointments to our

already beleaguered family. The winter had deposited record accumulations of ice and snow, followed by April's heavy downpours, ruining all the furniture and belongings we had in the garage. Tiny became very despondent, and once again turned to alcohol for solace, Uncle Charles joining him in his binges, fueling the already existing marital discord between him and Aunt Marge. Goo continued to pressure Tiny to find us a new house, lashing out at him, causing him to drink even more. We were caught in a vicious cycle of mounting frustrations, propelling us into frequent frights.

As if to signify all the outside forces poised to devour our family, large rats began assembling in the kitchen, leading to a bloody encounter between a foraging rodent and me one night. Restlessly tossing and turning, I had gone into the kitchen to warm up some milk. I had taken a stick with me, as I always did, so I could knock on the wall and let the rats know someone was coming into their area. But before I could perform this ritual, I saw what appeared to be a long dark shadow in the corner, illuminated by the light pouring through the window from a full pale-yellow moon shining between the limbs of an oak tree at the edge of the yard. I knew I had to act quickly, before the rat could stand up on its legs. One of our cousins had made the mistake of cornering a rat in his bedroom and gotten his cheeks and nose bitten.

The shadow began to rise and I swiftly pounded the huge old rat over and over and over with a stick, till the shadow swiftly descended back to the floor as his battered body fell in death. The next morning, Goo began pestering Tiny vehemently about getting us all into a safer house, blaming his recalcitrance for my coming dangerously close to having a gnawed-up face like my cousin. From then on, everybody was doubly afraid of going into the kitchen, especially at night, although none of us was ever bitten.

But all was not misery while at Mama's house. We continued to eat well, which was a blessing during these hard times. One white neighbor, Mr. Butler, provided Mama with venison whenever he came back from deer hunting. She learned to cook numerous creative and tasty dishes with his generous provision. Actually, Mr. Butler resided in one of the surrounding counties, but he owned a small garage, over which was a second-story apartment where he would spend a lot of time. I would go over to visit him sometimes, and we would talk about car engines or I'd listen to hunting stories. I soon added him to my growing list of friends from other ethnic backgrounds.

It was also while living with Mama that I began to use sunlight as my natural alarm clock. Due at the grocery store every morning at 7 a.m. that spring and summer, I automatically woke up each morning the minute the sun hit my eyelids. As fall brought in unceasingly dreary skies, I prayed to God to help me to continue waking up with the sun, regardless of how bright or dim the light. With His help, I woke up with each sunrise, or close to it. This helped enforce to me that God's light is always there and if we will just pray for help, He will keep us aligned with it.

When school started, I transferred to George Mason, located ten blocks from our home. Unbeknownst to me, I had been placed in a group of academically advanced students. I felt my old shyness coming back with these new classmates, many of whose parents were professional folk, skilled workers, or homemakers. They all had fancy lunch boxes, or enough money to purchase lunch daily, and here I came with my brown bags containing sandwiches wrapped in wax paper. Some of the boys rolled their eyes and prettily dressed girls giggled behind their well-manicured hands. Highly embarrassed one afternoon by the large grease stains covering

147

my bag (Goo had run out of wax paper), I ate my lunch in the hallway rather than endure the predictable taunts I'd receive if I dared enter into the cafeteria. So that evening at the store, I used my meager wages to purchase a silver-colored lunch box, allowing me to dine more comfortably with the others.

But these were minor jabs compared to the teasing I got about my too-large shirt and baggy pants, second hand but clean, given to me by Uncle Jack and Goo. I had worn new sweaters, slacks, white shirts, bow ties, and shiny new shoes while at Bellevue, so this second-hand dressing was a big step down for me. To my mind, I was sticking out like a scarecrow from the class row of well-tailored pupils, who either ignored me disdainfully or laughed out loud. But despite my sensitivity to this initially chilly reception, I was very grateful for these clean clothes, and realized my family had provided me their best during the difficult times we were experiencing. It made me proud to be part of such a loving, resourceful family, and I began not to care what my classmates thought about my apparel.

Ironically, as they began to sense my new indifference, their jeering decreased, and I began to see that it was really just a handful who acted this way, that there were a lot of nice students who accepted me just as I was. I became friends with most of my classmates, despite only attending there one year.

One afternoon in science class, some of the boys and I were in the midst of an experiment creating compounds from elements when our experiment produced such strong and unbearable fumes that the other students were compelled to run from the room. We ended up running from the room ourselves, after opening all the windows to no avail.

Despite my hectic work schedule, I continued to make all As in school. And I even managed to make a new friend in the neighborhood. Juan lived a block from us on 21st Street. Dapper, well dressed, and extremely intelligent, he took music and tap dancing lessons, demonstrating all the latest steps for me in the schoolyard or on the sidewalk. I was intrigued by his style, and he was envious of my mathematical abilities. So we began to barter. I had noticed that Juan always brought a huge lunch, with all different kinds of thick meat sandwiches, homemade rolls, and big slices of pie. So I offered to help Juan in math, in exchange for one of those sandwiches, some rolls, or pie. This schoolyard wheeler-dealering landed Juan an A in Math, and much improved my "daily bread," from peanut butter and jelly or leftover chicken to roast beef or Virginia ham. (Actually, Juan had done fairly well in math on his own, but he always had to be tops in anything he pursued, which worked out well for me).

Though I was getting along with the boys now, my interaction with the girls continued to dwindle, due to my continuing shyness with the opposite sex. We were all at the age where reputation among peers was paramount, and although some of the girls would talk sweetly to me when no one else was around, as soon as their saddity clique arrived they would become haughty and sarcastic, leading me to wish they just wouldn't speak to me at all. I began to avoid the girls, ignoring the ones who smiled or tried to approach me for fear they would pull the usual switch-up routine once their friends arrived.

Then I met Drew. Beautiful Drew's father was away in the military most of the time, leaving Drew, her mother, and younger sister and brother to move by themselves into the house across the street one early fall morning. I had seen Drew coming out of the house on a Sunday morning, her soft black curls cascading around her heart-shaped face, falling almost to the shoulder tops of her pink dress. She carried a black vinyl pocketbook, and wore pink hose and black patent leather shoes. I stood in front of our house, longing to go over and talk to her, but I just stood there staring as she entered the backseat of the Ford with her brother and sister, whisked off to church by her pretty mother, who smiled and waved to me as they passed.

Imagine my surprise when come Monday morning Drew walked into class, resplendent in her royal blue dress, causing sleepy heads to rise up, the boys craning their necks to get a glimpse of her, the girls admiring her snappy outfit. She sat at the desk right across from me, turning suddenly and giving me a heart-melting smile. I swallowed hard and managed to smile back, wondering if her friendliness would fade as soon as she entered into one of the popular girl circles.

Since it was the first day, the teacher took us through the usual recitations of summer vacations, and then she asked each of us what we planned to be when we grew up. Each student was required to stand up as they shared their dream with the class. One boy wanted to be a lawyer, another a carpenter. Maria Adams, snooty as the day is long, said she wanted to be a doctor (I already pitied her patients), and my ladylove wanted to be a teacher.

Finally, it was my turn, and I stood up, a bundle of nerves, as Drew was watching me intently. Taking a deep breath to calm myself down, I confidently asserted that I wanted to be an actor—just like Sidney Poitier, I added. Several students laughed, but it didn't matter to me, because at the mention of his name, Drew beamed at me approvingly, and I sat down as if on a cloud. It turned out that he was her favorite actor also, and he clenched my entry into a budding friendship between us.

That evening, I stood before the mirror, practicing moving like a panther, just like Sidney did in *Raisin in the Sun*.

"Who are you supposed to be?" Jamie asked derisively from behind me.

"Sidney Poitier, stupid."

"You look more like Goofy," she snorted.

But I paid no mind, continuing to watch my graceful moves in the mirror, planning to emulate them next time I saw Drew.

The next morning, I left to go work, not expecting to see Drew this early. I crossed the street, just so I could go by her house. I looked up at the second story, wondering which room was hers, imagining her sleeping in a bed with a canopy, in a pink nightgown, her hair flowing freely on her pillow. Suddenly, the front door opened, and out stepped Drew, to take in the morning paper and milk. Inwardly startled, I retained my outward "cool," and began easing down the sidewalk as I'd been practicing all last evening.

To my dismay, Drew started laughing. "What are you doing, Willie?" she called to me. Mortified, I proceeded to walk normally up the street, never looking back, thinking I had just ruined all my chances with her. I dreaded going to school, and now regretted that she sat right across from me. After debating whether or not just to go on home after work, I decided it was best to face Drew and get it over with. So I walked on to school, spying her standing in the yard with another girl as I approached. Uh-oh, here it comes, I thought as I passed them, waiting for the whispers, the giggles. "Hello, Willie." Drew smiled, then told her friend she'd see her in class, her cue to be left alone with me.

I stood there, not knowing what to say. She looked at me seriously. "Willie, about this morning—" She hesitated. "I like Sidney because he's—well, he's Sidney—" She waited, letting her words sink in. "And I like Willie when you're Willie! You see?"

Relieved, I nodded yes, and I walked her to class—minus my Sidney move. Drew continued to treat me kind and nice publicly and privately, giving me a much-needed boost of confidence. Soon I was a frequent visitor at her house, sitting on the porch, playing in the yard with my new "girlfriend," under the supervisory but approving eye of her grandmother, who would sit rocking on the porch, sewing or "just resting," as she would say. Drew is one of the happiest memories I have from this time at Mama's house, a wonderful girl who cared enough to make the extra effort with a shy boy.

October arrived, invigorating us with its cool, crisp air and dazzling leaves, prompting my friend Scottie and me to frequent the nearby Chimborazo playground. We were running, jumping on the piles of leaves, when some older boys we knew jumped on top of our prone bodies, their hand in our jacket pockets, in search of any change or bills we might have on us. When they came up empty, they got up and decided to let us go.

Scottie and I made a pact to retaliate, running to our respective homes, Scottie going to get a gun, while I planned to sneak out Uncle Buck's knife from his dresser. But for some unknown reason, neither Goo nor Scottie's parents would let us back out of the house that day. It was as if they knew already about the playground incident—it never ceased to amaze me how quickly grownups learn things. Whether someone saw and got the word to them while we were en route, or they were responding to our angry, trouble-bound eyes, I'll never know—but thank God our plan was foiled.

I had done well academically, made new friends, and had a new girlfriend by the time the next summer rolled around. And Uncle Jack bought me some suits to wear to school that following fall, so I actually looked forward to entering junior high school.

I also acquired a new adversary at the store, an older youth named Simon, who was tall, very intelligent—an honor student in school—and very light-skinned, what we called "high yellow." Mr. Price had made Simon my intermediate supervisor, and this taller, wittier, more aggressive boy teased me unmercifully, upsetting me emotionally to the point where I would become very angry and ready to fight. One day, he began calling me B.B., which was short for Boston Blackie (that was also the name of a white television detective at that time, but of course, Simon was referring to my darker complexion). I walked around the store upset for the rest of the day, ineffective in doing my work. Simon had won.

Mr. Price was amazed at my unusually sloppy performance that day, and he took me aside to find out what was going on. I related the name-calling, and he looked at me long and hard. "Willie, don't you know why Simon calls you names?" I shook my head no. He sighed. "Because he knows it will upset you, and you'll get angry and can't do your work! Just ignore him next time—and the next, and the next. And you know what? He'll get bored and stop calling you those names. Just try it and see if it works!"

So as difficult as it was, the next day when Simon called me "B.B." first thing in the morning, I simply ignored him. He kept trying to get the old rise out of me for a while, and I noticed that each time, it was getting less and less difficult for me to restrain my emotions and show no response. Simon, in turn, gradually stopped calling me names, just as Mr. Price predicted. Whatever subsequent problems I had with Mr. Price, I'll always be grateful for the lesson in reverse psychology he taught me that day, a lesson that held me in good stead whenever I encountered subsequent emotional abuse.

Mr. Price also schooled me about the use of the word "nigger," which was unfortunately used unflinchingly by many whites at this time. He told me that "nigger" referred to anyone with bad character, regardless of skin pigmentation. I took him at his word, and one day I availed myself of the opportunity to teach one of our customers about this word also.

The dog days of summer had just started when our regular bread salesman came into the store to make his delivery. I began counting the breads and pastries, but since he preferred dealing with Simon or Mr. Price, he pretended not to understand what I was saying. I continued to try to communicate with him, but he very gruffly told me to "get on, boy." Remembering my discussion with Mr. Price, I called him a "nigger," since that was how he was acting. His bespectacled chalky white face turned red as a beet, and he glared at me with an expression that I read as, "Who in the world is this little 'nigger' talking to?" Mr. Price was extremely surprised and stood behind the counter watching me in amazement as I casually went back to bagging an order as if nothing had happened.

The salesman wanted Mr. Price to dismiss me. The whole time he was concluding his business with Mr. Price, he kept turning around and glaring at me. They began speaking in lowered tones, and I know he wanted Mr. Price to fire me, or at least give him the satisfaction of seeing me disciplined. He left the store sorely disappointed, as Mr. Price never spoke to me about this incident. (After all, he was the one who had informed me that anyone could be a "nigger.") And the salesman suddenly could understand my speech the next time he made a delivery!

When I had first gone to work for Mr. Price, he had asked me if I had a middle name, which I didn't. So he explained it was best to have one, to minimize the chances of identity confusion. I used the name "Willie Thomas Woodson" to open my first Christmas club at a local bank. Each week, I would deposit $2.50 into my account to help my mother with Christmas expenditures. I also used some of the money to buy gifts for my sisters and brothers and for Mr. and Mrs. Price and their older son, Donnie, and younger son, Milton.

Mr. Price taught me not only how to read the stock market paper, but also the horse racing paper. And as I grew older, he took me along with his sons to Shenandoah Downs, Pimlico, and Marlboro racetracks whenever feasible. He had good insight when it came to picking winners, and when he got a hunch that a long shot would win the race, he'd close the store that Saturday and take off for the track, coming back to Richmond with a ticket for large winnings. So to keep from paying a large amount of taxes, he'd ask Mr. Johns, who lived behind the store, to go back to the track and cash in the ticket, giving him a generous stipend for this errand. He always told me it was the same way in any successful business—you had to play your hunches.

He also showed me the value of flexibility when dealing with challenges and opponents. I dabbled in boxing at this time, and was set to have a friendly match with Paul, a friend who was left-handed. So Mr. Price volunteered to train me as a southpaw boxer, which took my rival by surprise and allowed me an out-of-the-blue victory. I used this newly acquired dexterity to overpower Simon in an impromptu match the next week.

Meanwhile, my adeptness on the job had increased to the point where Mr. Price, when leaving the store to go on one of his jaunts to the racetracks, would leave me in charge, under the "free rein" supervision of his older son, Donnie. Donnie was a VPI graduate married to a Richmond Public School teacher. Saturdays were always our busiest days, and

I worked rapidly, simultaneously establishing genuine rapport with all our customers, being careful to always inquire about health, family, and special life events they had shared with me, so that young or old, they would leave the store feeling valued as a person, not just as a dollar sign.

I continued to eat well, Mr. Price and me taking all kinds of meat from the case—everything from steak to hot dogs—and cooking them in aluminum foil on a gas heater. (I had gotten so familiar with meat amounts that I could accurately assess what the meat would weigh before I placed it on the scale.) When some of the meat would get old, we would give it to the Johns family to cook before it reached spoilage rather than just throwing it away.

Some Saturdays, Mr. Price would send me to a restaurant at 23rd and Marshall streets to buy steak and egg sandwiches for our breakfast, but I wasn't hungry one morning, so I didn't buy one for myself. Mr. Price got very upset that I had turned down his offer. The whole family was like that—they didn't like to see you turn down any offer of food. Had I not been so very active and athletic, I would have been a stout youth rather than stocky and muscular!

Mrs. Price, who was from Roanoke, was a whiz at Southern cookery, and baked all kinds of pastries for us to eat. She also served me a heaping plate of her home-style cooking whenever she invited me over to their home on 4th Avenue, which was a completely white neighborhood at the time, though I never experienced any trouble during my visits. After dinner, I would sometimes tutor Milton, a student at John Marshall High School, as he was having trouble with algebra. His asking for my assistance bolstered my confidence in being just as intelligent as any other student, regardless of race.

Mr. Price purchased a red wagon, which I used to make

deliveries to some of our customers. They weren't obligated to give me a tip, but deep within me, I would expect that tip, and was extremely disappointed whenever it wasn't forthcoming. One of my favorite customers was Mrs. Jackson, a very light-skinned woman who was always polite and kind and gave me a substantial tip. One day, the Jacksons purchased oil and coal, so I eagerly took my wagon and made the delivery, expecting to see Mrs. Jackson's friendly face as the door opened, only to be greeted by her snooty daughter, who roughly and wordlessly took the goods from my arms.

I had seen her before, but she had always shunned me, never speaking, always a look of disdain on her face, shooing her three children back into the kitchen when they ran in to look at me, laughing and pointing. (Apparently, she was secretly afraid they might want to play with the numerous darker children around. It was rumored their father was white and she definitely kept them sheltered from most, if not all, of the other black children in our neighborhood, teaching them to show the same kind of contempt for us that she herself did.)

Not only did she not give me a tip that day, but she also shut the door in my face without so much as a civil thank you. I left feeling glad that she "sheltered" me from her brood, not wanting to acquire by association the rudeness and arrogance she was surely instilling in them!

Despite the good times I had with Mr. Price and his family, and the sound instruction he gave me in various areas of life, there were other times he would make me boiling mad, and I would up and quit, only to have him hire me back, after slowly taking his time to do so, a recurrent pattern that became as regular as clockwork. One such incident involved Mr. Sonny, a much older black gentleman who worked at the grocery store, who was considered a "wise old man" in our community.

Six feet tall, bald, bent over with age and hard work, he suffered with a hernia, but most of the time you'd never know it, as he seldom complained. He smoked a cigar and drank denatured alcohol, which we called "solocks." Mr. Sonny told me something one afternoon that resulted in my first of many immediate walkouts on Mr. Price, whom I had gone to the previous day requesting a raise, which I felt I amply deserved. He had turned me down without comment.

But that next afternoon, Mr. Sonny pulled me aside and informed me that Mr. Price had confided to him that he hadn't given me my raise because he didn't want me getting "nigger rich," explaining that this was supposedly when a black man had a little amount of money, thinking he had a lot. "Black doesn't attract anything but lint" was a similar common saying among whites then, meaning dark black men attracted neither women nor money.

I was furious as I had been ostensibly treated well by all the Prices and was too young to realize the extent to which racism could contaminate even the seemingly closest of relationships. But there we were, trapped within its constricting coils, neither one of us able to escape its insidious stranglehold. Yet I was also young enough to think I could extricate myself from this tenacious serpent's clutches with one bold exertion.

"If this is what he thinks of me, then I quit," I simply and firmly told Mr. Sonny, taking off my apron, walking out the door, leaving a line of customers staring pop-eyed at my retreating back. (He never knew why I quit, as neither Mr. Sonny nor I ever mentioned my knowledge of his comment.) I came back to work later that month, and the quit-comeback merry-go-round continued till I graduated from high school.

Despite his initial unjustness in granting me my raise—which I did obtain later, after my walk-out forced him to reconsider—Mr. Price had taught me in other ways to treat others fairly, and paradoxically, had even planned to sponsor my matriculation at Virginia Union University, though military duties precluded my being able to accept his offer. So the sting of his vast misconceptions about black people was partially mitigated by his extremely generous proposal. Still, despite my continuing gratitude and affection for the Price family, I couldn't dismiss the countless fellow victims of racism, whose anguish was in no iota offset by any such kind of benevolence; nor could I pretend to myself that the threads of presumed white superiority woven into the fabric of our relationship didn't exist.

Chapter 5

Finally, my family achieved what we had craved for so long during our odyssey of zigzag transplants, trying to make the best of diverse temperaments clashing in cramped quarters, in an attempt to avoid facing the underlying pain and bewilderment at the loss of Demi. Ever since we left 318 North 22nd Street, home had eluded us—until we moved next door to a restaurant between Marshall and Broad. Within the walls of this two-story wooden house, wounds healed, tempers settled down, and hope began to blossom like a flower sprouting beside a dusty, noisy road in a verdant patch of earth.

Our home was roomy, with a wide backyard sparsely covered with grass. A coal stove heated the large living room, rendered downright elegant by a crystal chandelier hanging from the high ceiling and damask drapes at the window. Felicia and the two older girls each had their own room upstairs, where I shared another bedroom with my brother, while the baby continued to sleep with Goo and Tiny.

I didn't care for the heavy, honking traffic constantly whizzing by, but we were directly on the bus line, so it was more convenient getting to school and work. Parallel to the restaurant was a bridge connecting 21st and Marshall, so we had easy access to Church Hill, the Medical College of Virginia state hospital, as well as to the downtown area. Goo was encouraged by the family to continue selling alcohol, so she did (their initial reluctance had faded as much-needed revenue poured in).

I continued doing well in school, despite all the domestic transitions. Although I'd been very nervous when first attending George Mason, the school had devised a plan in which students would form smaller groups and quickly get to know each other better. Each assigned homeroom class went as a group from one class to another during the day, establishing a feeling of unity as students bonded and formed friendships. This eased the transition from various neighborhood schools to one where all the different sections of the East End were represented—George Mason Community, Fairmont, Bellevue, 23rd Street, 21st Street, downtown Bottom, and 17th through 21st streets.

The next year, when I was in eighth grade, I transferred to East End Junior High School. This is why I was so glad Uncle Jack had purchased for me that previous summer seven new, well-fitting suits, so I could look as professional as many of my new fellow students surely would. He also saved me from having to fulfill my vow to myself that I'd use all the money I made at the grocery store to buy new clothes, even if it meant going without other more needed necessities—anything to keep from roaming the halls draped in the way-too-long Goodwill shirts and baggy pants I'd been wearing (although in current teenage fashion code I'd be right in style!).

I always have a special place in my heart for Uncle Jack, purchasing all those suits for his shy nephew who needed the extra boost in confidence at a time when acceptance by peers is so crucial. (I remember crying at the beginning of one year in elementary school because we didn't have enough money to purchase for me the requisite white shirt, bow tie, and sweater.)

While at East End, I attended all advanced classes. I also

had exposure to politics when I served as business manager on the campaign team for president and vice-president of our class. As incentive to potential voters for my candidates, I purchased candy from the grocery store; we designed name-etags, cards, and boards for our candidates, and helped with some of the forums. All the hard work and hustle assured our subsequent victory: Linda Smith and Carroll Terrell won respectively as president and vice-president of our class. This was the beginning of a lifelong love of and participation in the local political scene.

But I was not always "Mr. Exemplary Student" at East End, and I had more than my fair share of mishaps. For one thing, I was repeatedly late getting to history class, which was taught by the formidable Mrs. Gray, who on one dreary, rainy November afternoon handed me a note to be passed on promptly to Mr. Norrell, the physical education teacher. I wanted badly to open the note, but she had taped it with several strips, and I knew Mr. Norrell would duly report any tampering to her.

So I handed him the note, watching his poker face as he opened it, and growing more curious as to its contents. He then quietly informed me to bend down and hold my knees, as he was going to give me ten licks with the paddle, per Mrs. Gray's instructions. I was furious that I had been used to deliver my own sentence to the executioner. I swallowed hard, shaming as the two classes of girls and boys stopped their exercises and all stood watching me with amused eyes, waiting for the first blow, which came down suddenly on my backside, stinging my flesh as the expected hoots and hollers from the class filled my ears. Mr. Norrell, a natural-born sadist, waited a painfully slow moment before delivering the second lick, continuing at a snail's pace till I received all ten licks, and allowing the class to continue howling at my discomfiture.

I straightened up stiffly and limped into the hallway, show-ing no emotion, knowing any display would elicit further ridicule. But as soon as I reached the hallway, I broke down into tears, rubbing my burning backside with my hands. Then I wiped my tears away, straightened my clothes, and returned to class, passing the note to Mrs. Gray, who made sure it had been signed by Mr. Norrell, indicating that he had fulfilled her request. I sat in subdued anguish, barely listen-ing to her lecture on the French and Indian Wars, enduring classmates sneaking looks at me every time she turned and listed another battle on the blackboard. I was sore with Mrs. Gray for a long time, but in retrospect, I realized her disci-pline sprang from a bedrock of love, and the spanking had been rendered in fair judgment of my habitual tardiness.

Next year brought me to Armstrong High School—mighty Armstrong. Every East End boy dreamed of being a Wildcat, every girl of being escorted by a Wildcat to the prom. Ev-ery year, folks from all over town—and out of town—would flock to the football games between Armstrong's Wildcats and their rivals, the Green Dragons from Maggie L. Walker High School. The rivalry between these black high schools was phenomenal; and always the game that was played the Saturday just after Thanksgiving packed them in, with the highest attendance at a state sporting event for that time. The excitement that crackled through the crowd when the teams emerged onto the field was beyond belief, rising with the waves of fancy-threaded fans who jumped and cheered with each gain, falling back onto their seats in despondency with each fumble.

It had always been my dream to be a Wildcat. Maxi Rob-inson, history teacher, basketball and football coach, a true local legend, had seen me playing football on the Armstrong playground in a game sponsored by the City Recreation and Parks Department. I was thrilled when he talked with me about my potential and what an asset I'd be to the team. But when we approached Goo, my dream was shattered. She explained to Coach Robinson that I couldn't play because I'd had my appendix taken out as a child, and she was afraid any slight injury might provoke great physical harm to me. As I listened, each word was like a stab to my heart. I knew once Goo made up her mind, there'd be no changing it. I know she acted out of my best interest, but it galled me not to be on the high school team—especially since I did play some ball with the freshman players in the park and for the Mosby playground team, so I knew I was just as skilled, if not more so, than a lot of the others, and this made me feel a part of all their success. I attended all the games and proudly wore my orange and blue, our school colors.

There was a fierce school loyalty in those days that somehow has faded over the years. I was genuinely proud to be attending Armstrong, which has a long string of illustrious graduates, including former Virginia Governor Lawrence Douglas Wilder, and former Richmond Mayor Walter Kinney. Founded as the Richmond Colored Normal Institute in 1873, it was renamed in honor of Union General Samuel Armstrong, founder of Hampton Institute. It originally housed its students at 21 East Leigh Street in Jackson Ward before eventually moving to the large campus at 31st Street in Church Hill.

Being a big fan of rhythm and blues, I was especially proud that the Jarmels, who sang the nationally acclaimed "A Little Bit of Soap," hailed from Armstrong. Originally the Cherokees Quartet, one of their members was Dr. William H. Joyner, who had been a top athlete at Armstrong, principal of three city schools, including Armstrong, and was currently serving as head football coach at John F. Kennedy High School.

So my latent shyness sprang forth as I walked the crowded and bustling halls of Armstrong that first fall. My job precluded me from joining any extracurricular activities where I could have made friends more quickly. So I worked, studied, played football at the park when I could, and secretly noticed a bevy of beautiful girls strolling the halls in cliques, girls who were not paying much attention to the new boy unobtrusively noting every detail of an embroidered tight sweater or each feature of a pretty face, down to the shape of the lips or length of the eyelashes.

Swirling around us as we waded through the rushing autumn days were crashing currents of change routing us with their rapidity. Sputniks began orbiting the earth, and there was talk of sending a chimpanzee to the moon, and eventually a man. I listened intently to these stories of space travel being broadcast on radio and television, wondering if one day a black person would get to make the trip to another orb.

Then we all held our breath as Fidel Castro shouted threats at President Kennedy on the nightly news during the height of the Cuban Missile Crisis. I didn't understand all the ramifications involved in this ugly situation, but I knew with Cuba's proximity to our border, either destruction or resolution would occur quickly. We continued nervously watching their verbal wrangling, immensely relieved when Khrushchev finally ordered Russian missiles withdrawn from Cuba.

Then came a supposed reconciliatory period with Russia, as Nikita Khrushchev invaded America with a saintly smile, beaming at Mickey Mouse as he paraded by at Disneyland. He made quite a splash across our screens, even entering a line of the popular television show, "Car 54, Where Are

You?" ("…There's a scout troop short a child; Khrushchev's due at Idlewild…"). Then he flew back to Russia, vanishing as suddenly as he had appeared in America's spotlight.

One afternoon, I sat wistfully gazing at the fetching but snooty girl sitting across from me in history class. Just as I mustered the nerve to whisper to her to pass me a stick of gum she'd just slipped from her purse, the principal's sonorous voice thundered over the P.A. system: President Kennedy was dead—shot in Dallas, Texas. We were dismissed home amidst shock and bewilderment, our young eyes tearing at Mr. George Peterson's brief but compelling announcement.

I arrived at an empty house with a tear-drenched face, turning on the small black and white TV to gape in disbelief as Walter Cronkite continued to herald to an awestruck people that their smiling vibrant leader of just this morning was dead. That very next Sunday, we watched his alleged assassin, a very young, small, white male, gunned down amidst a large group of press and Dallas's finest.

A short few weeks later, Jerry Rustin ran into my drafting class stopping beside me out of breath and shaking his head. Jerry was scheduled to be in his electronics class next door, so I supposed someone in his family must be hurt or dead. But surely it wasn't the name he murmured—not Sam—no, he didn't say Cooke.

Elegant, handsome Sam radiated a spirit that grabbed you when you were at your lowest and set you on your feet again, ready to reenter the fray of life, with the weapons of tenacity and faith filling his songs. Whether wistfully crooning the joys and disappointments of young romantic love, or vocally salving the wounds of daily dashed hopes and dreams left to fester within his people, Sam made it known by the end of each song that he would make it—and made you believe you would make it, too.

And he grew wings and soared above it all when he led the Soul Stirrers through the old familiar stories of healing and comfort found in the darkest night, at the end of the longest, hardest road, within the loneliest broken heart. Whenever he came to town there I was, sitting at the Mosque amidst all the fluttering females surrounding me, some caught up in the spirit, but others caught up in Sam's handsome face as he looked into their eyes with his when he stepped forward to solo.

Shot down last night. In Los Angeles. Impossible. Jerry has something wrong—they'll operate, get the bullet out, I told myself as I ran through the door that evening, cutting on the TV, watching its images flash in the darkened living room. They confirmed my friend's report—a plain, middle-aged portly black woman sat looking into a CBS camera, telling the world ever so casually, ever so unremorsefully, that yes—she had shot Sam dead. Had to, she said. He was chasing the girl, trying to rape her, she said. That's all there was to it—the woman disappeared from sight, replaced by Cronkite with the latest news on one of Lyndon Johnson's daughters' romances. I turned off the set, and went upstairs without eating supper.

I turned on my radio, and Sam still lived, his voice serenading me, as the deejay played tune after tune in honor of Sam. This went on till about midnight. The years fell away—the deejay mixed early gospel songs by the Soul Stirrers with Sam's smooth solo ballads, haunting bluesy numbers, and rockers, such as the recent "Shake." And every hour on the hour, they played the song that had become the unofficial national anthem of Sam's people—"A Change Is Gonna Come": "I was born by the river," he told me, "been running ever since," he sang—but now the flow had ceased.

But not the sound of that brief refreshing wave that had lapped over my dry and empty recesses. I heard the rolling wave rising again on each mellifluous note. With the vocal trumpet Sam had been given as a voice, he had called forth all the hidden longings and pains I wasn't even aware I contained, cajoling me to face them, to use them as the fuel for my own resolve, rising up and burning steadily, torched by his own fervor till we became a conflagration of flame. That was the beauty of Sam—cool water or smoldering spark—whatever was needed, he could dole it out.

Sam took any kind of music and transformed into it his own style, without losing a scintilla of the original feeling. Down home "Little Red Rooster," teenage angst "Another Saturday Night," even the old country standard "Tennessee Waltz"—all became uniquely Sam's. Now "Touch the Hem of His Garment," now "Steal Away," came gloriously flowing out of the radio by my bed, even after Sam had stolen away—or been stolen—it was all a bad dream—I would awaken—

I woke up late the next morning, tardy for work and dashing for my clothes. Sam was gone, but the busses were still running, people still needed groceries. And all day the radio continued to nourish our souls with Sam's voice. We had to make it now—we had to do it for Sam.

Rumors circulated—the girl he was chasing was a prostitute—they had left a party together and gone to a fleabag motel in Watts—he'd caught her trying to lift his wallet from his pants pocket—he'd chased her unarmed to where she fled for protection—to the "madam"/manager of the motel, the steely-eyed matron of the newscast who shot him—it was later reported he looked up at her and whispered, "You shot me, lady," as stunned as we were at her cold-bloodedness. There had been no arrests, no interminably long trial a la

O. J. Simpson. We heard nothing of any further or pending investigation. I hated this woman, free to carry on without impunity in her own nefarious obscurity, after so cavalierly extinguishing our brightest flame.

Jet, Ebony, all the local black newspapers duly carried the tributes, the unanswered questions, the young widow's face stoically gazing off into the distance—burying her husband now—she and Sam had buried their drowned seventeen-month old son the previous year. How did she feel about this reported fatal liaison? Had there been other entanglements? But now, Sam's childhood sweetheart, Barbara Campbell, was Sam's wife no more—and like the song that Sam had written and recorded back in 1963 said—though at the time, it went unreleased—she, like the rest of us, had to "keep movin' on."

But all wasn't sadness that fall. In between the death of Kennedy and Cooke, everyone managed to get caught up with the Walker-Armstrong game, which took place the Saturday after Thanksgiving. I was returning from watching the guys practice, going down the school corridor past the display case next to the library, when my own drafting caught my eye. A third place ribbon was attached to the upper right-hand corner of my drawing of a chimney, and though I was overjoyed that my creative work was valued and shared by the school population, to this day I have no idea how or why my work was selected. One of life's enjoyable mysteries.

Then Saturday arrived, the day of the big game. As usual, I had to work, so I had to be content with listening to all the fanfare on the store radio. Because most of our regular customers were going to the game, business was crawling. Passing the store was a slow-rolling cavalcade of cars, bedecked with orange and blue or green and white ribbons flapping in the cold November wind, inching down Broad Street on their way to City Stadium. Spirited groups congregated at the bus stops, a fashion show of sharp coats and trousers, exquisite fur-trimmed hats, and shapely silk-stockinged legs tucked into two-toned spectator pumps. Some of the crowd began arguing about who would win—a good deal of this was good-humored banter, but there were many heated exchanges as well.

Families divided on this day, including my own. My father, one sister, and I cheered for Armstrong, while Goo and another sister rooted for Walker. We had ribbons of both school colors hanging all over the house, and had teased each other unmercifully all week that each respective alma mater would be the winner.

For one day in the year, a football game that was much more than a game brought the black community together in a much-needed buoying esprit de corps, reinforcing the reality that individual accomplishment is entwined with community advancement. Underneath the surface rivalry, unity and loyalty were being solidified. We were as one, and the striving of one became the striving of all. The residual effects on our community of this electrifying rally, this one glorious galvanizing day, cannot be overemphasized. But, as with all the other football and basketball games, I would not attend, relegated to watching the same crowds through the store window that I would later hear cheering on the radio. I was a senior before I finally was able to attend this classic game. It was the pinnacle of my last year at Armstrong.

Besides sports, music was my prime passion and we listened to all types at the store, engendering in me an appreciation for all its various expressions. Tiny continued to listen to classical at home, and Mr. Price would often play a classical station on Saturdays. My growing familiarity with the works of various composers allowed me to fully savor the symphonies played by the Armstrong High School Orchestra at our assemblies.

Tiny and I always watched Lawrence Welk together on Sundays, and we enjoyed watching the dapper host doing an exuberant polka with a sprightly lady chosen from the audience. He also relished Nat King Cole's rich delivery, as did Mr. Price, who often played big band and jazz on the store radio. Nat's wording was so clear and distinct, which appealed to me also (Sam Cooke followed in Nat's steps in this regard, stressing the importance of well-enunciated lyrics to all the artists he worked with as producer at his SAR Records studio).

We also listened to contemporary stations, which were filled with songs by the Beatles, the lately imported British hurricane blowing all the American artists off the top of the charts. I watched them storming onto The Ed Sullivan Show, looking funny to me with their soup bowl haircuts and Nehru jackets. But the girls in the audience saw them differently, and it amused me to watch the camera zoom in on a host of screaming young female fans, closing their eyes in ecstasy, pulling their long hair straight out from their heads.

Ed Sullivan was highly appreciated by black viewers, as he alone among all the variety show hosts would devote entire shows to black artists. These showcases afforded us the rare treat of seeing all our favorite singers, dancers, and comedians on television, whose landscape was colored a dominant white. And many Southern whites hated these shows, complaining to CBS that Sullivan was a "nigger lover." But Ed was immensely popular, and persisted with regular all-black revues, as well as frequently including black performances on other shows.

As Motown ascended to the heights of the charts, giving the King Beatles a run for their money, Ed hosted all the major Detroit artists, such as the Supremes, and my favorite from the Motor City, Stevie Wonder. James Brown was a frequent guest also, and we would all go see his shows so we could get our dance moves together. He stopped by Richmond often, so we were able to stay at the top of our form. Everyone copied James.

It was also while living on 21st Street that I went to the racetrack with Milton and Mr. Price for the first time. I was extremely excited about this new venture, as I had heard Mr. Price having many discussions with Donnie about his bets. Every morning he'd go through the same ritual—buy a Morning Telegraph and Washington Post from the bus station, then dig in immediately to his homework, giving keen and arduous contemplation to the background of horses and jockeys, as well as current conditions at the various tracks.

So that morning, we were on our way to what I'd only heard about for several years. Arriving at the Marlboro track, I was overwhelmed at how vast a crowd was milling about. We went to place our bets, and after much consultation, we decided which tickets we wanted to purchase. So while allowing us to feel we had a part of the decision, Mr. Price actually swayed us to agree with the choices he, as a "professional" playing for much bigger stakes, knew were best.

We sat in the stands, eager for the horses and their riders to appear. I marveled at the size of the jockeys, diminutive on the backs of the brawny horses of all colors. Just watching the powerful horses run around the track, skillfully mastered by their tiny riders, was fascinating. Suddenly, the horses began slowing their pace, and I thought something was wrong, leading Mr. Price and Milton to chuckle at my naiveté. They explained that a small mirror was placed at the finish line, and the race was ending as the horses came to a halt at this line. Then they both jumped up and whooped, me along with them, as our horse was first to the line. Mr. Price bought us all hot dogs and sodas to celebrate, and this was but the first of many exciting days at the races.

Getting to Armstrong was also a very interesting excursion some days. Uncle Jack didn't drive us to school anymore, but the bus stop was right across the street from our house, my job affording me the privilege of buying bus tickets, so getting to school was actually no hardship. But I wanted to play a bigger part in my friends' doings, so I often walked three blocks down Jefferson Avenue to meet my group, Jerry, Snagi, Buster, Egg, and Lonnie—a star of our group, as he was quarterback of the football team. Work so often prevented me from hanging out and having fun with the guys, so any chance I got to participate in whatever they had going on, I took it, including this ritual of hitchhiking to Armstrong.

Our strategy was for one or two of us to stand at the corner of 25th and Jefferson, and when a car stopped for the red light, they'd motion for the driver to give them a ride. If he agreed, the rest of us, hidden behind a nearby house, would all run out and jump into the car also. The driver, overwhelmed by the sudden appearance of all these boys—and not wanting to hold up the line of drivers behind, who by now were impatiently honking and yelling out their windows—would usually succumb to all the pressure and drive on, although several furiously vowed to contact either our parents or the police about this. Surprisingly, we never experienced any repercussions.

One morning, the much larger Lonnie tried to keep me from getting into the car, as there were really too many of us for the backseat. The door of the car was open, and the driver, already frantic over what had taken place, sat frozen behind the wheel, waiting for the light to turn. Lonnie and I fought with the door still open, the other boys cheering us

173

on. The light changed, so I plunked down hard on Lonnie's lap as we rode along Nine Mile Road. One of my friends pointed out that my upper lip was now bleeding, which I hadn't even noticed, as my mustache covered the injury and I felt no pain. When the principal saw me, he stopped us and asked what happened to me. The other boys eyed me nervously, wondering if I'd squeal, but I told him I'd fallen and landed face down, as I didn't want to get our star quarterback kicked off the team!

My friends also persuaded me to play hooky with them one day. They did this frequently, but I'd never done it before. Buster Chris (his real name was Keith) lived in a set of apartments across from the brand new Mosby Middle School. So on a bone-chilling rainy winter morning, Jerry, Egg, and Snagi decided to go over to Buster's place instead of to Armstrong, as his mother was always away at work during the day. After much coaxing, they convinced me to come along. We hung around the apartment till lunchtime, then went across the street to Mosby to eat in the new cafeteria. We would have stuck out like sore thumbs from all the younger children, and surely Mosby's principal would have made a call to ours. So I persuaded the other boys to walk up to Dunkin' Donuts on West Broad and have our lunch there. We sat at the counter, shivering from the cold rain we'd just walked through for blocks, and that piping hot coffee and those soft, sweet, warm donuts tasted extra good. But that was my only enjoyment from this jaunt, and I never played hooky again.

Another time, my love of always dressing "clean" kept me from getting into hot water with Mr. Peterson. Armstrong had a very strict dress code—shirt, trousers, and shoes required for boys, skirt and blouse or dress and shoes for girls. But this particular day had been preplanned by the senior class to be "Triumphant Day," when all seniors would wear tee shirts, jeans, and sneakers. I was impressed with the catchy and original name chosen for this endeavor, but not with the idea itself.

I always wore a suit, shirt, and tie, sometimes sweater and dress slacks, and didn't relish the idea of coming to school looking sloppy (to my mind). I guess it all stemmed from the days when we didn't have enough money for me to be neatly attired, so it's always been important to me to look sharp. So after ruminating all night before, I decided that morning to come to school attired appropriately as always. As I approached the building, I saw large groups of students leaving the school. Several of them told me Mr. Peterson was sending every senior home to change into acceptable attire and return within a certain time limit, with a signed note from their parents, so he could make known to every family what had transpired and inform them that it wouldn't be tolerated in the future. I was the only senior who didn't have to go home and explain why to my family. It felt good to be the only one not in trouble that time!

So being a good Armstrong student saved me that day, but being from Armstrong landed me in a fight another day. I always tried to take the earliest bus possible from school so I could have some time to relax at home before going on to work. One of these earlier buses was always full of students from Fulton, another rival area. I caught this bus that afternoon, the only Armstrong student in a sea of stony, sneering faces.

I sat near the center exit door so as not to have to walk through this unfriendly group. My regular heckler, Lou, loud and very obese, started in on me as usual from the rear. I had so far ignored him, being outnumbered, but this afternoon I'd had enough, and he riled me to the point that I threw all caution to the wind, springing up and running back to him, pounding on his head with my fist. The stunned Lou just sat there in complete silence, as I prepared myself for a group jumping me, although I was angry and determined enough to take them on regardless of the consequences. To my astonishment, everyone started laughing at Lou, and not one student rose up out of his or her seat to defend him. Apparently, his own crowd didn't care for him either. I went back to my seat, leaving the beaten and embarrassed Lou to sit there hanging his head in pain and shame. When I got off the bus, the Fulton students whistled and applauded, which bolstered my confidence, that I had stood up for myself despite overwhelming odds and gained respect. I rode the same bus the rest of the week, and a silent Lou had to endure all the razzing he'd been giving to me.

Dealing with my mother's selling liquor was also a continuing struggle for me, one I couldn't win. I knew she had to have a livelihood to make ends meet for a family of seven. Uncle continued to help us meet bills as much as he could, and Tiny's income from shoe repair was most insufficient. But it galled me to see the patrons disrespecting our home and taking advantage of Goo's kindness. With drink in hand, they'd ask for permission to use the phone, dialing already before permission was vocalized. They'd settle back on the couch and rest their feet on the coffee table, something we were never allowed to do. Worse still was the way they took food from us.

Goo always cooked a meal fit for a king, even on weekdays. Weekends, we sold dinners to the patrons, me helping minimally with preparation in between shifts at the store. The kitchen was a bedlam of activity, with gamblers playing at the table amid folks queuing for dinners. But folks would often wait until Sunday evening to request a meal, knowing this was when Goo was way too liberal giving away food to whoever was present. This irritated me to no end, more than anything else the customers did. I would ask Goo time and again why she tolerated all the disrespect—she didn't from us. She would never dignify my query with a verbal response, but her silence loudly sent the message to me, "Be quiet."

Home to me was where family lived and enjoyed life, with respect for each member as well as anyone else who entered the doors. I had been thrilled to get a room with my brother, where I would think and dream and plan in quiet and solitude. Now it was a dim memory—I was forced to tolerate a noisy, boisterous gathering in our home all through high school. Adding to my frustration was the chagrin that always rose in me every time I got off the bus near our house, knowing everyone knew it was a "liquor house." I eventually trained myself to block out what others thought, but deep inside, it still troubled me. I became even more determined to make more money, so Goo and the rest of us would have to endure all this upheaval no more. I used to bemoan the way I had to hustle when I was young, missing out on so many good times with my friends. Now I see it was a blessing come in disguise, as blessings often do, because it taught me early to make the most of every opportunity, every moment that comes my way. And I do.

While in high school, I continued to be assigned to all advanced classes. Then in my junior year, I decided to withdraw from these classes, as I did not appreciate the disdainful attitude my peers displayed towards the average and academically challenged students. In elementary school, my good grades never affected my behavior outside of school with my less scholastically successful friends. So at Armstrong, I continued to make a conscientious effort not to let my academic achievement turn me into an intellectual snob.

So when I recognized this type of mindset and behavior within the "advanced group," I no longer wanted to participate (although I didn't inform my parents of my decision until after that school year). And though I made the honor roll every report period, I didn't even realize it until I read about myself in the school newsletter. (I was too busy working and being a regular guy to notice each school recognition.)

I thank God that He instilled in me an affinity for the oppressed and underachievers at such an early age, but with the hindsight of maturity, I realize I made a mistake dropping out of the advanced classes, which I could have continued to attend while simultaneously supporting other students. But at the time, I had an "either/or" mindset, which caused me to misconstrue opportunity for influence with betrayal of my friends.

Many of my neighborhood friends were older than I was. I guess having to go to work so early in life matured me beyond my years. We were an eclectic bunch, which kept things hopping. Wesley had polio, Bumpy, though singularly unexpressive, was quite a communicator with his fists, while Randy was the mild-tempered, smooth lover of the group. Then there was Murphy—heavy, jovial, intelligent, and a born comedian. Melvin was macho and considered himself a step ahead of Casanova, although in reality Randy had him beat. Since Ed had one brother and five sisters, he had an easy camaraderie with the opposite sex, although often he ended up being cast in the role of the confidant or big brother rather than romantic leading man. He was an avid reader and was also designated the intellectual among us.

At the other end of the personality spectrum was Massenburg, the no-nonsense all-business man always coming up with creative ways to generate much-needed greenbacks in a timely fashion. He was also the one who originated a fraternity for us neighborhood boys, designing the colors and emblem as well as devising the charter and rules. Also, he, Ed, and a couple of other boys brainstormed and came up with our fraternal name, as well as many ideas for get-togethers, among ourselves as well as with the opposite sex.

I was excited to be part of this group, as belonging greatly enhanced my social skills. We were required always to conduct ourselves as gentlemen, and our reputation as such spread among the girls, affording us a calling card with some of the brightest and prettiest misses in town. Three of my fraternity brothers' most spectacular conquests were sisters who resided on Clay Street, in the Jackson Ward section of the city. Classy and sophisticated, all were light-skinned with long, straight, coal-black hair. The short, small-featured sister was seeing Ed, the tall, full-figured one was Wesley's choice, while Melvin dated the curvy one of medium height.

We would all go trooping over to their houses together, as their parents were always chaperoning, so no one frat brother could go alone, as this would have been disrespectful. I was envious of their success á l'amour, and decided this was the kind of girl I would eventually be fortunate enough to date. I watched how they interacted with the three sisters and made mental notes for future reference. Imperceptibly, the fraternity disintegrated our last year at Armstrong, as we all began heading in different directions. The girls moved to another section of the city and Massenburg began pursuing his business aspirations by landing a job as a mail clerk, while I continued working at the store till graduation.

One summer at the store, an altercation took place that ended in a bizarre scenario in a storefront church. Peter—tall, skinny, poorly groomed, often reeking of body odor and the stale, smoky breath he always blew in your face as he approached (he had started smoking when he was a child)—came into the store in one of his frequent foul moods, itching for a fight—and finding one with me. Peter had a dry, sarcastic wit, though he was by no means an intellectual, and he had a habit of needling fellows with his sharp tongue till they grew hot and took the desired swing at him. This was his way of getting the fight he wanted whenever he became frustrated with life, habitually provoking stronger fighters, then relying on his lightning speed to escape from his opponents before they could seize him and beat the stuffing out of him. He had been waylaid several times by fellows still steaming over being cheated of their licks, but he had never learned his lesson.

So we started off exchanging a few mock insults, then he began roughly playing around, lightly wrestling around the soda case. Things quickly got out of hand. He became more boisterous with his holds and jabs, then I became more aggressive and backed him against the drink case, exerting a lot of pressure on his arm and throat. Suddenly he pulled a bottle of coke out of the case and stunned me with a hard hit behind my right ear.

After the hit, I was ready to kill him, so I chased him out of the store down Broad Street, as I held my ear that was throbbing and burning like the whole side of my head was on fire. He crossed the street rapidly amid moving traffic, looking over his shoulder at me, as I kept calling to him that I intended to slaughter him. His eyes were wide with fear, and he increased his speed like a racehorse galloping to the finish line, but I was behind him all the way like proverbial white on rice.

Suddenly, he did something I wouldn't have had the gall to do—nor would just about any guy in our neighborhood. This coward actually ran inside a small red brick building that, unbeknownst to me, was used as a church in the front, while a family used the back part of the building as their living quarters. So I chased Peter, grabbing for his shirttail, barely missing my opportunity to drag him back out in the street, before reeling with shame and embarrassment before the startled members, who stood in the sanctuary frozen over their hymnbooks, gazing at us in amazement, their joyous song was silenced by this entrance of what they surely must have deemed a couple of lunatics. I stopped in my tracks, like a man running down a dark alley, making out the brick wall at the end just in time to brake before crashing head first against it.

Peter ran through the little assembly of worshippers and out a rear door. Though I was not a churchgoer at this time, Mama had instilled respect for God in me, and I refused to make any further mockery of His sanctuary. I didn't speak to the members, mostly older folk, as some of the women began shaking their heads at me, their eyes mighty censures as they stared straight into mine. I wanted to beg their forgiveness but my tongue was stuck to the roof of my mouth, so I lowered and nodded my head, silently pleading for pardon, then turned and quickly exited.

"Just a Closer Walk With Thee," their time-worn but robust voices sounded again, as I stood outside the sanctuary, my ears pounding as Mama's face suddenly appeared before me, an angry prophetess beating me down with her fiery eyes, just as her sisters inside had wordlessly done. I shut my eyes against her vision, and still holding my smarting ear, I walked slowly up the hill to the store, sorely disappointed that Peter had gotten away, but not regretting my decision to let him.

I returned to a very angry Mr. Price, who interrogated me as to what kind of emergency prompted me to leave in the middle of work. I related the entire sorry episode, as he smirked at me and shook his head, sternly warning me not to pull such shenanigans at the store again. So I channeled all my frustration with Peter into my work, actually getting more done than normal. The resilience of youth is amazing, and when Peter returned to the store several days later, my desire to harm him had dissipated and we were friends again. We both laugh about this experience to this day.

Goo was largely responsible for my acceptance of folk others labeled "undesirables." Though the backyard parties she and Uncle hosted could get rough and rowdy at times, they taught me a lesson in valuing all sorts of people, with all their quirks and foibles. We lived on a street mainly consisting of hard-working folks with a strong sense of being good neighbors. And these were the kind of people who mostly attended our family parties. But there were also some "middle-classers" who would stop by to party, and they freely mixed and mingled, glad to get away from the corporate grind and the rigid rules imposed on them by the arbiters of social decorum among their set—rules we saw as being laden with hypocrisy and pretension.

At our parties, they could partake of a more democratic social atmosphere, where the rules were more basic and flexible. The main requirements for everyone were not to disrespect anyone else and not to create a disturbance or nuisance that would attract the police. We also had customers from the restaurant next door to come over and join the festivities, so we always had an interesting mix of revelers.

One night, an untidy, musty-smelling drunk came off the street into the yard and began eating the food and helping himself to good liquor, after which he joined several unescorted ladies in a fast dance. He acted as if he were an honored guest, which infuriated me. I immediately went over to where he was, dipping one of the ladies who was tipsy and laughing, waiting for him to release her so I could direct him to leave the yard.

But I felt Goo's hand on my arm, pulling me over in front of the shrubbery where we could talk. She reminded me that we were to respect everyone who came, whether or not they were the same social class or status as we were. Then she went over to the man, who was walking away, thinking we had decided to send him packing. She warmly embraced him, assuring him that he was welcome to stay and enjoy himself. The look of relief and gratitude on his face made me see his humanity, and I felt ashamed of my attitude and behavior. I went over and shook his hand, complimenting him on his steps with the two ladies, which were actually pretty good. Thanks to Goo, who was kind and wise enough to welcome the stranger, I have always done the same.

Despite my being a prize pupil with most of my teachers, all was not well in academia. Of all people, my homeroom teacher—a most important figure in the instructor lineup— had an aversion to me—why I never knew—which she had no qualms about showing at every opportunity. Since her treatment of me was not in response to any bad behavior on my part—she just plain didn't like me—I didn't endure her abuse in silence, which was the root cause of the only D appearing on my report card. I felt it was highly unfair and unprofessional for a teacher to abuse her power this way, playing favorites and undermining students not cared for. I had decided that the next time she verbally let me have it in front of my classmates, I would verbally give her both barrels back—and loudly, for all to hear.

This particular morning, I was late for homeroom class, which naturally prompted a barrage of too-personal insults from the salty Ms. Spi. Initially, I calmly requested that she not disrespect me. It was fine with me to be disciplined for being late, but I was tired of her personal assaults. But she screeched at me to "sit down and shut up" because I made her sick to her stomach. That did it. "Make you sick to your stomach?" I blurted in frustration. "How do you think you make me feel when you keep giving me Ds I in no way deserve?"

She turned ashen, pursing her lips and glaring at me with what was supposed to be her most intimidating scowl. But I had had enough and wasn't backing down, even if it meant being expelled. Next, she tried threatening me with a higher authority. "I'm going to tell your mother!" she said slowly and evenly through clenched teeth.

"Good! Because I'm tired of you being so unfair! Her number is 643-3221. Call and tell her right now!"

"I'll call her at a time I'll decide, Mr. Smarty!" she thundered back. "Now take your seat!"

I sat down amid a heavy silence. No one dared defend me or even so much as snicker, as no one wanted to incur the wrath of Ms. Spi the year of graduation. Then when I got home that evening, Goo called me into the kitchen and asked for my version of the reported incident. Since this unruly act of mine could have resulted in me not graduating in May, Goo instructed me to apologize to Ms. Spi and admit I was wrong to "backtalk her." I couldn't believe she wanted me to go before all my classmates and eat crow to a teacher who was so rude and so wrong.

But, under orders, the next morning I approached a huffy Ms. Spi and apologized, though I did it quietly, hoping none of the other students would hear me. But the pupils in the front of class overheard, and immediately titters ran up and down the rows, as Ms. Spi stood beaming, reprimanding no one for laughing, which she normally would have done. She savored my discomfiture till the bell mercifully rang. After all my talk the previous day, I was the joke of the class, but I endured it, as now I would be able to graduate on time.

But I wasn't out of the woods yet. Upon giving an oral presentation in another class without benefit of note cards, I was surprised to be scolded by the teacher who took the lack of cards as an indication that I hadn't adequately prepared for my talk. I disagreed vehemently and pointed out that my thorough exposition of the material proved I had prepared so very well that I didn't need notes to prompt retention of the information. My plea fell on deaf ears, and her attitude caused me to lose enthusiasm for the course, and I never performed well in her class after such discouragement of my hard work.

So when it was time to look on the board to see if I had graduated, I walked the long way around the school building with Snag, Egg, and Buster, my heart pounding. We maneuvered our way through the throng of students, positioning ourselves at the front near the board. To our great relief, we had all passed and we all jumped towards the ceiling, hugging each other and running out of the building, whooping, tears of joy running down our faces. At home, Goo informed me she knew I was going to pass all along, but was asked by Ms. Spi not to tell me. Guess she wanted for me to sweat it out to the very end.

But any wounds from skirmishes with buddies and teachers were nothing compared to the hard knocks love gave me all through high school. Misguided entanglements presented themselves in dizzying sequence, starting in a full-blown affair with an older woman while I was but a sophomore. This very attractive lady had approached me at the store one evening, under the scolding eye of Mr. Price watching the encounter from behind the cash register. She complimented me on my mustache, while pronouncedly scrutinizing my muscular arms with her soft brown eyes. After she left, my surrogate father admonished me sternly, detailing all the perils involved in pursuing such a relationship at my age—especially since the lady in question was sporting a huge diamond wedding ring.

I didn't think anything of her flirting at first, figuring it was just that and wouldn't develop into anything more, but each time she returned to make groceries, we would talk briefly, Mr. Price continuing to evil-eye us while we made arrangements to meet discretely, which I knew was wrong, but with my continuing bashfulness with girls my own age, I was very vulnerable to this experienced paramour's ego-boosting attentions.

Once we got going, I had a hard time emotionally extricating myself from the web of deceit we were secretly weaving. We called ourselves being in love with each other, so we continued to rendezvous with blinders on, till eventually I managed to take mine off and face the inevitable dead-end crash to which we were headed. So I continued to meet my ladylove, while inwardly preparing a tactful exit from our arrangement, provided for me when I was called to military duty.

While this was covertly going on, I was openly attending concerts at the Coliseum, where there were plenty of pretty girls enjoying all the big-name singers who came to town. I didn't get off work until Saturday night, but often I would head for the Coliseum, at 1st and Clay streets, where the show would last until two or three in the morning. But I had to be home by midnight, as Goo wisely denied me a key to the house on the nights I went out. Zee helped me out by staying up and opening the door for me so I could stay out till closing time. Taxi fare was $1.95 from the Coliseum to our house, so I always made sure I was left with enough money for the fare, after paying for my entry fee and spending for drinks (non-alcoholic).

One Saturday night, just as spring settled softly on a city finally rousing itself from a dreary and debilitating shroud of continuous cold March rain, I exited the yellow cab that had pulled up to let me out just as the show was starting at the Coliseum. The warm air had me feeling frisky, even prompting me to tip the driver, a rare occurrence in those times. I got my ticket and strolled inside, trying my best to look nonchalant as I mingled with the mostly older teenagers and young adults, striking a blasé expression in hopes of disguising my glaring juvenility.

A sudden tap on the shoulder had me turning around to look into a pair of emerald green eyes warmly glowing in a porcelain face, framed by golden ringlets flowing down to the shoulders of a blue taffeta blouse filled neatly by a pleasant-looking, though not exactly pretty, white girl. She beamed me her radiant smile, seemingly unaware of my surprise at seeing her there as I retained my insouciant demeanor.

She looked old-fashioned standing amid the tight-sweatered, short-skirted bevy of girls parading around us, and when she asked me to dance, I hesitated, nervously envisioning the Martinsville Eight—the eight black youth who had been accused of raping a white female— walking past me in manacles, their features settled into stoic resignation, their eyes betraying lingering glimmers of pain. She stood there waiting for a response, her affable patience cajoling me into taking her arm and circling her around at arm's length amid tightly groping couples, my partner smiling and ignoring the icy eyes staring at us from all sides. My initial jitters returned as some of those eyes caught mine, and I quickly looked away, growing more and more embarrassed, although

I felt guilty for feeling so, as the girl was very nice, talking to me softly as we danced. She told me her name was Jerri, which intrigued me as I'd never heard of a girl with that name before.

At the end of the set, I released her with a slight nod of my head and a meek smile, retreating to my perch by the wall. In retrospect, I wish I'd ignored my peers and asked her to dance again. But I was hungry enough for social approval — and rightly enough concerned for the trouble we would have landed in at that time and place — often deadly trouble — that I let her walk away. She tried to conceal her obvious disappointment with a quick gracious smile in my direction before turning, unknowingly paining me to have to let her take that walk, another casualty on the racial battlefield we had briefly tried to negotiate.

I stayed until closing time, watching the shows, the dancers, the lovers, through a fog of swirling smoke rings that tickled my throat and stung my eyes, prompting me to sporadic coughing fits. Jerri had left earlier and I only danced a few more times, contenting myself to unobtrusively people watch, a pastime I continue to relish.

I had more than enough for the cab fare home, as I'd only consumed a few sodas. Way past my curfew as usual, I wasn't worried, as Zee would have my back. A light was on up in the girl's bedroom when we pulled up in front of the house, so I climbed out of the backseat and quietly eased up the front walk, waiting on the porch for Zee to come down and let me in. The door finally opened, and I smiled at Zee, who stepped aside to present me with an angry Goo, who boxed my ears.

"How stupid do you think your mother is, boy? I've been knowing about your little Coliseum capers — I've been too worn out to stay up and catch you sneakin' in — but I'm bushy tailed tonight, and you fell right into my trap, mister."

She turned around and surveyed her daughter looking at the floor, her hands folded. "And you know what's in store for you, next time you let your brother sneak in this house!" She turned back to me. "And neither one of you buzzards got any way of knowing when the hen's gonna be up prowling this here barnyard! So be careful you don't ruffle these feathers again!"

With that, she boxed both sets of stubborn ears, turned and bounded up the stairs without a backward glance. That was the end of my midnight forays, and I disciplined myself to get home by 9:30-10:00 at the latest—exerting all the will power this night owl could muster.

Because I was frequently burning both ends of my candles, I would end up falling asleep at work, either sitting with my eyes closed on the coal pile, or disappearing into the restroom for long intervals. Mr. Price finally had enough of this, and gave me a lecture about not letting nocturnal socializing interfere with the next day's work. I knew that as long as he saw me standing up, he would figure I was okay and on the job. I trained myself to catch brief snatches of sleep standing up, relaxing my shoulders into a comfortable posture, locking my knees into bent position, and leaning my body against something firm. Five minutes sleep here and there was a deliverance, even for a healthy youngster like I was, staying up till 3 a.m. and getting up at 7 a.m. to get ready for work. After I fell snoozing onto a fruit stand one morning, almost breaking my jaw, I learned to stand over piled sacks of flour, assuring me a soft landing should I fall over again!

Meanwhile, I was falling in love with all the frequency youth allows. After dallying with my older lover, then dancing with a girl considered "taboo," I continued to swim in waters over my head—and prom night was no different. This time, I was more than happy for everyone to see me with the dream date I had landed—or thought I had landed.

I had initially asked Mary, a pretty, sweet black girl with soft, smooth ebony skin, one of the smartest girls in class but very down-to-earth and friendly to everyone, regardless of class or social group—which I admired. Many of the pretty girls at school developed stuck-up attitudes. But Mary was different, and I was pleased—though a little surprised—when she said yes to my request. Then I pulled a real boner—one I still regret.

An extremely popular, so-called sophisticated (really, just snooty) light-skinned girl named Velma began cutting around me all of a sudden. (I found out later she was using me to spite a college boyfriend, who had broken up with her shortly before the dance, depriving her of the opportunity to show off a handsome college beau to the other girls). Foolish enough to be struck by her fair skin, I left my Nubian princess in the lurch, with a sheepish but callous admission that I had decided to go with someone else, so she needed to get someone else to take her to the dance. Hurt and angry, she showed real class by walking away from me like the dignified queen she was, leaving me to enjoy my short-lived fantasy of taking the "better" girl to the prom.

It was an intoxicating spring night, with a thousand sparkling stars floating in a cobalt-blue celestial sea suspended over fragrant front yard gardens, perfumed wide avenues lined with blossoming white dogwood trees. I sat in the backseat of my Uncle Thomas's black Cadillac, feeling like a king, dressed to the nines, a boxed white corsage for my ladylove in my hand.

As we pulled up in front of Velma's house, my heart started thumping in anticipation of seeing her in her gown. Her mother opened the door and motioned me inside. Her face was an older version of Velma's, but her figure was much heavier. Velma's father had died several years before, so I was spared the "who are you to take out my daughter" inter-rogation. Her mother was very cordial, and even brought me some iced tea to sip while I sat on the sofa waiting for Velma to calculatingly make her late grand entrance.

She appeared at last at the top of the stairs, pausing for effect, cocking her head slightly and preening royally. I watched her gracefully descend, taking out the corsage to pin on her dress as soon as she reached me. She was admittedly radiant in a white chiffon evening dress, which accentuated her tiny waist and full hips. I pinned the corsage on her low-cut bodice, my fingers trembling as they were dangerously close to her ample breasts.

She laughed, throwing her head back. "Actually, you should have handed me the box and let me do it—especially since you could have stuck me, the way your big clumsy fingers were shaking!" She said the words lightly, teasingly, but I found the crust underneath this slice of needling unap-petizing, and I wasn't about to have it dished out to me all night long.

I vainly tried to dismiss my foreboding, holding the door open for Velma, who kissed her mother on the cheek, then preceded me out the door. Her mother stood watching us from the doorway, sighing and smiling. "Daughter, you look just like I did the night your father pinned me. Willie, if I were thirty years younger, I'd have my hook in your fine flesh," she teased, as I escorted Velma down the walk to where Uncle stood holding the backdoor open for us, play-ing the chauffeur role to the hilt for our benefit.

She thanked Uncle sweetly, then sat way over next to the window, talking to Uncle, not saying diddly to me. I felt like a fifth wheel on my own date, but though set at low boil under my lid, I said nothing, while Velma kept chatting amicably with Uncle. He made several attempts to bring me into the dialogue, but I didn't respond, which seemed to suit Velma just fine. I didn't know what sort of game she was playing—I only knew she had picked the wrong mister to play with.

Uncle and I had made arrangements for me to call him after the prom was over so he could pick us up and take us to our respective homes, where we could change from formal to casual attire, as we were to attend a graduation party being held at a hotel later that night. So when he dropped us off at the Mosque—used as a theater for shows and for dances—he opened the door for a beaming Velma and a steaming Willie—though I didn't show it. I told him I'd call him later, thanked him for bringing us, then took Velma's arm, dutifully escorting her inside.

We sat at a table with some of my neighborhood friends and their dates. I had to sit across from Velma, as there were no two seats left together when we arrived. Our friends danced several sets, going and coming with enough frequency that I could have switched seats and sat next to my date at any time, but I stubbornly refused—nor did she ask me, or indicate to me in any way that she would have liked me to sit next to her.

Whenever my friends were at the table, she went out of her way to include me in the conversation, laughing and looking my way. But as soon as they all hit the dance floor again, she turned her back and started watching the dancers, leaving me sitting there virtually invisible and feeling like a fool.

I decided to make the best of the situation, as I'd been looking forward to this night for a long time. So I gave her the benefit of the doubt, thinking maybe she was simply being coy, waiting for the male to make the first move. As we sat at the empty table, her head turned to watch our classmates,

I asked her, "Velma, would you like to dance?" She turned around slowly, and stared at me blankly. "Willie, when I'm ready to dance I will let you know!"

Startled by her blatantly rude response, I made one of my own. "Okay—I'll be on the dance floor until you are ready," I informed her curtly. She gaped at me in surprise, apparently not used to guys standing up to her. Well, this sister didn't know who she was dealing with. I wasn't about to let her childish charade ruin this important evening, one which would never return to me again.

So I had a great time on the floor, dancing and laughing with classmates, many other pretty girls happy to dance with me. Out of the corner of my eye, I saw several other guys approach Velma, who turned them down flat. After that, there were no more takers, as I guess they assumed they'd just get shot down also.

Finally, I headed back to the table. Trying to still show respect, despite the fact that I had been accorded none, I asked Velma to dance one last time—and I meant it would be the last time. Now she said yes, and I held her at a proper distance through a slow ballad. She never spoke but just kept looking at me closely. Then she leaned over and whispered in my ear, "Willie Woodson, opportunity knocks only once."

I looked at her quizzically. "Opportunity for whom?"

She looked at me in disbelief. "Opportunity for you, fool! For a girl like me!"

Now I stared back in disbelief, beginning to think her arrogance was exceeded only by her ignorance. It was at this moment that I decided she was going home to stay when my uncle picked us up after the dance. We resumed dancing stiffly for a few minutes, then returned to the table, along with some of the other couples. Our conversation cruised along at the bare minimum, but in class spirit, we did pose for some pictures together, along with some of my closer classmates.

After the picture-taking, I resumed my basically stag stance, changing partners every few sets, till finally I ended up right next to Mary and her date, who had been across the floor from where I danced most of the night. I can't remember when I felt more shame and regret, as I endured Mary's date holding her closely through a slow dance. He was an attractive, intelligent guy (far more intelligent than I had been when I spurned her in pursuit of a lighter hue).

She never looked over at me—too gracious and ladylike to engage in any eye rolling or "rubbing in," which made me feel even smaller. For the rest of the night, I made sure I was way away from whatever area of the dance floor Mary and her beau were at. Velma finally broke down and danced a few times with other guys—although I never asked her again after the "opportunity lecture." She had lost her opportunity with Willie, who at least had enough sense to know he had just as much to offer as she did!

The prom ended, I made my call to Uncle, whom we waited for in mutual silence. He pulled up and I escorted a sulky Velma to the car, where Uncle Thomas, ever the gentleman, again held the door open for us. But this time, before getting in, I quietly informed my flabbergasted Uncle that we would be carrying Velma home to stay, giving him no explanation for the change in plans until after we'd dropped her off.

He drove away puzzled, Velma sitting in the back in stony silence. I politely escorted her to her door—she lived in public housing, so I especially wanted to make sure she got to the door safely at this time of night. I said good night, and as her mother opened the door, I turned and walked back to the car, went home and changed for the party, where I had a ball with my stag self!

About a week later, I received our prom pictures, and still wanting to be a gentleman, decided to take them to Velma. So I caught the bus, which let me out on the corner near her house. I rang the bell and her mother answered. When I told her I'd brought some prom pictures for Velma, I didn't know what her daughter had told her or how she would receive me. But she was very hospitable, inviting me in and offering me a drink, which I declined. Velma entered the room, most surprised to see Willie sitting on the sofa.

"I thought we'd seen the last of each other, Mr. Willie." She walked over and looked at the package lying in my lap.

I ignored her tartness. "I have the prom pictures, and thought you'd like to have them."

"Well, let's see them."

We looked at the pictures together, even laughed at the ones where some of my friends were clowning behind us. Then she dropped the ultimate question: "Why did you leave me at home and not take me to the party?"

"Because I'd had enough of the nasty attitude you copped for no reason — and I wasn't about to let someone who wasn't worth the agony mess up the prom for me — or the party with my friends." I expected her to slap me for the bluntness of my answer, but it had to be said.

But ever nice-nasty, she leaned forward and whispered a deadly taunt in a soft sweet voice. "The boys in this neighborhood worship my fine behind, and one wink of my eye, they'll beat you till you pray for death." Then she backed away, scrutinizing my reaction.

"Get any moron who wants to sign his own death warrant. I can take care of myself, sister. And my cousins in the next block can take care of themselves too." I mentioned their names, and she backed off, as my cousins were known as rough customers. In an attempt to placate me, she offered me a drink, which I again declined, dropping the packet of pictures on the sofa, then heading out the door to the bus stop, looking around in preparation of Velma's toadies suddenly approaching. But I boarded the bus without conflict—nor was there any later, despite her bluff. As far as I was concerned, the whole ugly episode was over, and good riddance to her.

But Mary continued to haunt me. I had recurring nightmares in which I'd go to a movie or a show and end up in line behind Mary and her escort. I made a vow, which I kept, never to two-time a nice girl like that again. For months, I tried to summon the courage to apologize to Mary and ask her forgiveness, but by the time I mustered my nerve, she had moved away.

While all these romantic dilemmas were going on, the Vietnam conflict had reached its zenith. As I was still a senior planning to go to college, I wasn't worried. Because of my excellent grades, coupled with financial need, I received a scholarship to Hampton Institute. Mr. Price overwhelmed me with the surprising and most generous offer of paying my tuition at Virginia Union for all four years. Buoyed on this wave of blessings, I came home from the store, opened the mailbox, and sank like the Titanic. There it lay in my hand, the long, thin envelope, the deliverance of which dashed all my dreams.

The Department of Defense, it read in the upper left-hand corner. Inside, instructions to fill out draft forms. I replied, expressing my interest in furthering my education, outlining all my opportunities, including the scholarship. They sent me another letter, ignoring my outline of my educational plans. They had other plans for me, and when I didn't respond to this second letter, they sent me a third, instructing me to report to Main Street for Army enlistment.

Since I had to go—quietly or kicking and screaming, Uncle Sam didn't care which—I decided I'd prefer the Air Force to the Army, so I went down to their recruiting office, explaining my situation to the recruiter, who told me I would need my high school diploma and a qualifying status on a test they'd administer before they could accept me. I told him I was graduating in May, and agreed to take the test. As there was a month's lapse between the date I was to report to the Army recruitment office and the receipt of my Air Force test results, the recruiter instructed me to inform the Army that I'd already taken the Air Force test and was awaiting the results.

But two weeks before I was due to report to the Army office, the Air Force recruiter called me and told me I'd passed their test with flying colors. Further, I was scheduled to leave Richmond that same week, bound for basic training in Amarillo, Texas. So I got a quick haircut, laughing at my bald self in the barber's mirror, then hurriedly packed an overnight bag with light clothing and toiletries.

I had never mentioned any of the letters to Goo, or any of my machinations for switching to the Air Force. Now, I didn't tell her about my impending departure, knowing she would be horribly upset about me going into the military, and possibly ending up in Vietnam right as President Johnson had escalated the bombings.

So I confided my orders to Zee, imploring her not to tell Goo, as I would call her from the airport and tell her myself. She honored our agreement, and the next morning, I washed up and ate a very small breakfast, catching the bus down to the Main Street Federal Building to enlist in the Air Force, pleasantly surprised to see my neighborhood buddy Jerry already waiting patiently to be sworn in. As it turned out, we were the only two of our group to enlist in the Air Force—all the other guys entered the Army.

After the swearing in, we were given a light lunch and driven to the airport. My flight wasn't leaving until late afternoon, so I had a long time to hang around and mull over how I would break all this news to Goo. In between perusing various newspapers and magazines and watching the many passengers come and go at the busy airport, I mentally rehearsed my hello-goodbye call to Goo, dreading the moment when I would have to drop the dime into the pay phone and hear her surprised and sad voice, for what could be the last time, for all I knew.

Fifteen minutes before departure, I dropped in my coin and dialed my mother, my heart racing, my palms dripping with sweat. I heard the click indicating that someone had answered, and Goo's happy voice sounded on the line. "Hi, Goo," I started out, trying to sound cheerful to soften the coming blow. "Guess where I am?"

She laughed, figuring I had just gotten myself into one of my local scrapes. "Out doing something you've got no business doing, what else?" She waited for me to join in the joke, but when she got no answer, she knew something was very wrong.

"What is it, son? Talk to me!"

In a low and broken voice, I blurted out that I was at the airport, headed for Air Force training in Texas in just a matter of minutes. There was silence, then a stunned Goo murmured softly, "Stop playing with me, boy."

"I'm not. My plane's leaving in a few minutes—I can't talk too long, because I've got to leave." I listened to Goo's silence, cutting into me like a sharp knife. Tears rolled down my face, and I rued not having had the courage to tell her face-to-face. We were only miles apart, but I might as well have been on a different side of the planet—and soon would be. "I'll call you as soon as I can. I've got to go now." I paused, but there was no answer. "I love you—pray for me." Still no response. I hung up the receiver slowly, bracing myself to make the flight that would sever me from my family, my friends, my dreams for four years, along with all the other boys severed from their homes by a war that made no sense to us. They announced the flight, so I stood up and walked resignedly out to the plane, boarding and taking a seat next to the window. I studied the long, skinny clouds threading lazily through the pale blue sky, the roofs of what now looked like dollhouses as we ascended over Richmond: anything to obscure my mother's face. I had to compose myself, had to halt the tears welling in my eyes, and focus on the task before me—getting my Air Force service behind me, and returning safe and sound to my home.

Four years later, I would return—safe, basically physically sound, but bearing emotional scars that would take years to heal. I left on a clear, beautiful spring afternoon. I returned to America in the aftermath of a hurricane that had rocked Virginia that morning. I had to hitch a ride down to Richmond from D.C., due to the weather conditions. Goo hadn't answered my frantic call from the airport, so I held my breath and prayed all the way that I would find her and our house intact when we arrived that night.

I hurried up the walk to the door of the still-standing house, knocking persistently several times. Goo opened the door, holding a fat white candle that illuminated her tired face, brightening at the sight of her son standing before her. She set the lighted candle back into its holder on the table, then hugged me tightly, our tears mingling as we pressed our wet faces together.

She picked up the candle, leading me upstairs to my room. I set my grip down next to the bed, watching her face, older, worn, glowing with joy in the soft candlelight. Then I sat on the bed and began singing "Every day will be like a holiday when my baby gets home." She took my hand as I sang, tears running down her face. I had written to her that I'd sing that song for her when I got home, as we had shared in our letters that we were both listening to it in different parts of the world, both anticipating blessed reunion.

I lay back in the darkened room relieved only by the small circle of light around Goo's face, trying to fight the over-powering fatigue that gripped me all at once. "That's right, you rest, baby. I'll get you a blanket—gonna be chilly to-night, baby—already October."

I watched the circle of candlelight move steadily down the hallway, outlining Goo's face as she turned and opened the closet door. I fell asleep as the light flickered and came back towards me, Goo's precious voice jubilating in the dark-ness—

"Beams of Heaven as I go—"